THE
MAYA

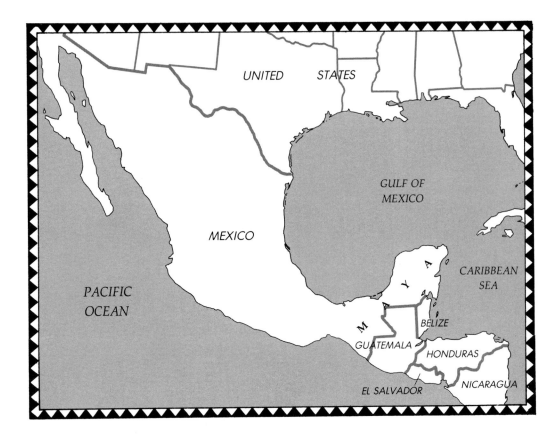

UNITED STATES

GULF OF
MEXICO

MEXICO

PACIFIC
OCEAN

M
A
Y
A

CARIBBEAN
SEA

BELIZE

GUATEMALA

HONDURAS

EL SALVADOR

NICARAGUA

THE
MAYA

Lawana Hooper Trout
University of Central Oklahoma

Frank W. Porter III
General Editor

CHELSEA HOUSE PUBLISHERS
New York   Philadelphia

On the cover A ceramic figurine of a Maya ruler wearing regalia of war. The sculpture was made between A.D. 600 and A.D. 800 and stands approximately 11 inches high.

Chelsea House Publishers
Editor-in-Chief Remmel Nunn
Managing Editor Karyn Gullen Browne
Copy Chief Juliann Barbato
Picture Editor Adrian G. Allen
Art Director Maria Epes
Deputy Copy Chief Mark Rifkin
Assistant Art Director Noreen Romano
Manufacturing Manager Gerald Levine
Systems Manager Lindsey Ottman
Production Manager Joseph Romano
Production Coordinator Marie Claire Cebrián

Indians of North America
Senior Editor Liz Sonneborn

Staff for **THE MAYA**
Copy Editor Brian Sookram
Editorial Assistant Michele Haddad
Designer Debora Smith
Picture Researcher Melanie Sanford

7 9 8 6

Library of Congress Cataloging-in-Publication Data

Trout, Lawana.
    The Maya/by Lawana Trout.
        p. cm.—(Indians of North America)
    Includes bibliographical references (p.) and index.
    Summary: Examines the history, changing fortunes, and current situation of the Maya Indians. Includes a picture essay on their crafts.
    ISBN 1-55546-714-8
        0-7910-0387-6 (pbk.)
    1. Mayas. [1. Mayas. 2. Indians of Central America.] I. Title II. Series. III. Series: Indians of North America (Chelsea House Publishers)   90-2309
F1435.T8 1990   CIP
972.8′004974—dc20   AC

CONTENTS

INDIANS OF NORTH AMERICA

CHELSEA HOUSE PUBLISHERS

INDIANS OF NORTH AMERICA: CONFLICT AND SURVIVAL

Frank W. Porter III

The Indians survived our open intention of wiping them out, and since the tide turned they have even weathered our good intentions toward them, which can be much more deadly.

John Steinbeck
America and Americans

When Europeans first reached the North American continent, they found hundreds of tribes occupying a vast and rich country. The newcomers quickly recognized the wealth of natural resources. They were not, however, so quick or willing to recognize the spiritual, cultural, and intellectual riches of the people they called Indians.

The Indians of North America examines the problems that develop when people with different cultures come together. For American Indians, the consequences of their interaction with non-Indian people have been both productive and tragic. The Europeans believed they had "discovered" a "New World," but their religious bigotry, cultural bias, and materialistic world view kept them from appreciating and understanding the people who lived in it. All too often they attempted to change the way of life of the indigenous people. The Spanish conquistadores wanted the Indians as a source of labor. The Christian missionaries, many of whom were English, viewed them as potential converts. French traders and trappers used the Indians as a means to obtain pelts. As Francis Parkman, the 19th-century historian, stated, "Spanish civilization crushed the Indian; English civilization scorned and neglected him; French civilization embraced and cherished him."

Nearly 500 years later, many people think of American Indians as curious vestiges of a distant past, waging a futile war to survive in a Space Age society. Even today, our understanding of the history and culture of American Indians is too often derived from unsympathetic, culturally biased, and inaccurate reports. The American Indian, described and portrayed in thousands of movies, television programs, books, articles, and government studies, has either been raised to the status of the "noble savage" or disparaged as the "wild Indian" who resisted the westward expansion of the American frontier.

Where in this popular view are the real Indians, the human beings and communities whose ancestors can be traced back to ice-age hunters? Where are the creative and indomitable people whose sophisticated technologies used the natural resources to ensure their survival, whose military skill might even have prevented European settlement of North America if not for devastating epidemics and disruption of the ecology? Where are the men and women who are today diligently struggling to assert their legal rights and express once again the value of their heritage?

The various Indian tribes of North America, like people everywhere, have a history that includes population expansion, adaptation to a range of regional environments, trade across wide networks, internal strife, and warfare. This was the reality. Europeans justified their conquests, however, by creating a mythical image of the New World and its native people. In this myth, the New World was a virgin land, waiting for the Europeans. The arrival of Christopher Columbus ended a timeless primitiveness for the original inhabitants.

Also part of this myth was the debate over the origins of the American Indians. Fantastic and diverse answers were proposed by the early explorers, missionairies, and settlers. Some thought that the Indians were descended from the Ten Lost Tribes of Israel, others that they were descended from inhabitants of the lost continent of Atlantis. One writer suggested that the Indians had reached North America in another Noah's ark.

A later myth, perpetrated by many historians, focused on the relentless persecution during the past five centuries until only a scattering of these "primitive" people remained to be herded onto reservations. This view fails to chronicle the overt and covert ways in which the Indians successfully coped with the intruders.

All of these myths presented one-sided interpretations that ignored the complexity of European and American events and policies. All left serious questions unanswered. What were the origins of the American Indians? Where did they come from? How and when did they get to the New World? What was their life—their culture—really like?

In the late 1800s, anthropologists and archaeologists in the Smithsonian Institution's newly created Bureau of American Ethnology in Washington,

D.C., began to study scientifically the history and culture of the Indians of North America. They were motivated by an honest belief that the Indians were on the verge of extinction and that along with them would vanish their languages, religious beliefs, technology, myths, and legends. These men and women went out to visit, study, and record data from as many Indian communities as possible before this information was forever lost.

By this time there was a new myth in the national consciousness. American Indians existed as figures in the American past. They had performed a historical mission. They had challenged white settlers who trekked across the continent. Once conquered, however, they were supposed to accept graciously the way of life of their conquerors.

The reality again was different. American Indians resisted both actively and passively. They refused to lose their unique identity, to be assimilated into white society. Many whites viewed the Indians not only as members of a conquered nation but also as "inferior" and "unequal." The rights of the Indians could be expanded, contracted, or modified as the conquerors saw fit. In every generation, white society asked itself what to do with the American Indians. Their answers have resulted in the twists and turns of federal Indian policy.

There were two general approaches. One way was to raise the Indians to a "higher level" by "civilizing" them. Zealous missionaries considered it their Christian duty to elevate the Indian through conversion and scanty education. The other approach was to ignore the Indians until they disappeared under pressure from the ever-expanding white society. The myth of the "vanishing Indian" gave stronger support to the latter option, helping to justify the taking of the Indians' land.

Prior to the end of the 18th century, there was no national policy on Indians simply because the American nation had not yet come into existence. American Indians similarly did not possess a political or social unity with which to confront the various Europeans. They were not homogeneous. Rather, they were loosely formed bands and tribes, speaking nearly 300 languages and thousands of dialects. The collective identity felt by Indians today is a result of their common experiences of defeat and/or mistreatment at the hands of whites.

During the colonial period, the British crown did not have a coordinated policy toward the Indians of North America. Specific tribes (most notably the Iroquois and the Cherokee) became military and political pawns used by both the crown and the individual colonies. The success of the American Revolution brought no immediate change. When the United States acquired new territory from France and Mexico in the early 19th century, the federal government wanted to open this land to settlement by homesteaders. But the Indian tribes that lived on this land had signed treaties with European governments assuring their title to the land. Now the United States assumed legal responsibility for honoring these treaties.

At first, President Thomas Jefferson believed that the Louisiana Purchase contained sufficient land for both the Indians and the white population. Within a generation, though, it became clear that the Indians would not be allowed to remain. In the 1830s the federal government began to coerce the eastern tribes to sign treaties agreeing to relinquish their ancestral land and move west of the Mississippi River. Whenever these negotiations failed, President Andrew Jackson used the military to remove the Indians. The southeastern tribes, promised food and transportation during their removal to the West, were instead forced to walk the "Trail of Tears." More than 4,000 men, woman, and children died during this forced march. The "removal policy" was successful in opening the land to homesteaders, but it created enormous hardships for the Indians.

By 1871 most of the tribes in the United States had signed treaties ceding most or all of their ancestral land in exchange for reservations and welfare. The treaty terms were intended to bind both parties for all time. But in the General Allotment Act of 1887, the federal government changed its policy again. Now the goal was to make tribal members into individual landowners and farmers, encouraging their absorption into white society. This policy was advantageous to whites who were eager to acquire Indian land, but it proved disastrous for the Indians. One hundred thirty-eight million acres of reservation land were subdivided into tracts of 160, 80, or as little as 40 acres, and allotted tribe members on an individual basis. Land owned in this way was said to have "trust status" and could not be sold. But the surplus land—all Indian land not allotted to individuals—was opened (for sale) to white settlers. Ultimately, more than 90 million acres of land were taken from the Indians by legal and illegal means.

The resulting loss of land was a catastrophe for the Indians. It was necessary to make it illegal for Indians to sell their land to non-Indians. The Indian Reorganization Act of 1934 officially ended the allotment period. Tribes that voted to accept the provisions of this act were reorganized, and an effort was made to purchase land within preexisting reservations to restore an adequate land base.

Ten years later, in 1944, federal Indian policy again shifted. Now the federal government wanted to get out of the "Indian business." In 1953 an act of Congress named specific tribes whose trust status was to be ended "at the earliest possible time." This new law enabled the United States to end unilaterally, whether the Indians wished it or not, the special status that protected the land in Indian tribal reservations. In the 1950s federal Indian policy was to transfer federal responsibility and jurisdiction to state governments, encourage the physical relocation of Indian peoples from reservations to urban areas, and hasten the termination, or extinction, of tribes.

Between 1954 and 1962 Congress passed specific laws authorizing the termination of more than 100 tribal groups. The stated purpose of the termination policy was to ensure the full and complete integration of Indians into American society. However, there is a less benign way to interpret this legislation. Even as termination was being discussed in Congress, 133 separate bills were introduced to permit the transfer of trust land ownership from Indians to non-Indians.

With the Johnson administration in the 1960s the federal government began to reject termination. In the 1970s yet another Indian policy emerged. Known as "self-determination," it favored keeping the protective role of the federal government while increasing tribal participation in, and control of, important areas of local government. In 1983 President Reagan, in a policy statement on Indian affairs, restated the unique "government is government" relationship of the United States with the Indians. However, federal programs since then have moved toward transferring Indian affairs to individual states, which have long desired to gain control of Indian land and resources.

As long as American Indians retain power, land, and resources that are coveted by the states and the federal government, there will continue to be a "clash of cultures," and the issues will be contested in the courts, Congress, the White House, and even in the international human rights community. To give all Americans a greater comprehension of the issues and conflicts involving American Indians today is a major goal of this series. These issues are not easily understood, nor can these conflicts be readily resolved. The study of North American Indian history and culture is a necessary and important step toward that comprehension. All Americans must learn the history of the relations between the Indians and the federal government, recognize the unique legal status of the Indians, and understand the heritage and cultures of the Indians of North America.

A fragment of a carved stone panel from a temple at the Classic Maya site of Copán. The carving depicts the ruler Yax Pac (First Dawn), who came to power in 763 and was Copán's last recorded king. He is seated on a now-lost throne and holds an offering dish in which lies the head of God K, a symbol of the ruler's divine leadership.

1

ORIGINS
AND
SURVIVAL

The thread of Maya history stretches from antiquity to today. Many ancient and modern Maya believe their history began with the creation described in the *Popul Vuh, the Quiché Book of Counsel*.

In the beginning, all was calm. There were neither humans nor animals, birds nor fishes, trees nor stones. There was only the calm sea and the empty sky. Only the Creators Tepeu and Gucumatz were in the bright water hidden beneath green-and-blue quetzal feathers. Then spoke Heart of Heaven: "Let the water recede! Let the earth appear! Let there be light!" Like a mist came creation. Mountains grew from water. Cypress trees put forth roots into the earth. But the Creators knew there could be neither glory nor grandeur until humans appeared. First, they shaped humans of earth, but these beings were limp and their faces fell to one side. They spoke, but had no minds. So the Creators destroyed them.

Then the Makers told Grandmother Dawn, "Cast the corn, cast the lot with your grains and read if we are to make beings of wood." Grandmother Dawn cast her corn and read the divination: "It is well that figures be made of wood." The Makers spoke, and instantly wooden figures appeared. But their faces were dry and crusty, and their bodies had no blood or heart. The wooden beings did not praise their Creators and were destroyed. Rippers of Eyes tore their eyes from their sockets, Killer Bats snatched off their heads, and lurking Jaguars ate their flesh. A rain of darkness began and a great flood fell on the wooden ones.

Then the Creators said, "Let beings appear who will praise us." From the spreading waters came the yellow-and-white ears of corn. From this sacred maize, the Creators made the flesh of humans. These first humans were Jaguar Quiché, Jaguar Night, Nought, and

Wind Jaguar. They had perfect knowledge, but the Creators knew that mortals should not see too far, so Heart of Heaven chipped their eyes. Thus, these first Maya became the ancestors of modern Maya according to the *Popul Vuh*.

The *Popul Vuh* preserves sacred and secular Quiché Maya history. Ancient priests told its stories through generations. Later, scribes recorded the histories in hieroglyphic picture books. Finally, after the Spanish conquest, Quiché lords learned to write their language using the Roman alphabet. They wrote the *Popul Vuh*, which appears today in Mayan, Spanish, English, and other languages.

The *Popul Vuh* revealed the pattern of cosmic order in the Maya universe. Creation set forces in motion that defined the Maya way of life. First, the gods shaped the land to which the Maya remain tied today. Maize, gift of the gods, nourished the people. Thus, the cosmos was a partnership between gods and humans. Humans praised the gods, who in turn provided their children's earthly needs. The ancient Maya paid tribute to the gods by sacrificing their blood and sometimes their lives. Today, descendants of the ancient Quiché live in highland Guatemala where priests consult cosmic order to interpret omens, dreams, and rhythms of time. These diviners, called Daykeepers, cast their lots to bring knowledge. Daykeepers determine children's names, wedding dates, and other important decisions.

Since the beginning of their civilization, Mayan people have sought harmony between their daily lives and cosmological forces. Religion has affected all aspects of their lives. Today, approximately 5 million Maya, speaking 1 of the 30 Mayan languages, still live on their ancestral homeland. The modern Maya, however, live in traditional communities and in cities in Mexico, Guatemala, Belize, Honduras, and El Salvador. As direct heirs to more than 4,000 years of history, cosmology, and traditions of their forebears, contemporary Maya struggle to preserve traditional ways against pressures of 20th-century life.

The Maya homeland of approximately 125,000 square miles is one of the most varied environments on earth. It divides into the lowlands in the north and the highlands in the south. A great backbone of volcanoes dominates the highlands, which have yielded vital resources. The ancient Maya quarried obsidian—volcanic glass—for making sharp tools and developed lively trade in obsidian, jade, and other precious materials. Another volcanic material used as grinding stones (*manos* and *metates*) was basaltic rock. Although steel cutting-tools have replaced obsidian ones, the Maya still use the traditional basalt mano and metate for grinding maize and other foods. At home in the highland rain forest is the rare quetzal bird, prized by the ancient Maya for its brilliant green plumes and revered by the modern Maya as the national bird of Guatemala. Millennia of rain and ero-

REGIONS WITHIN THE MAYA HOMELAND

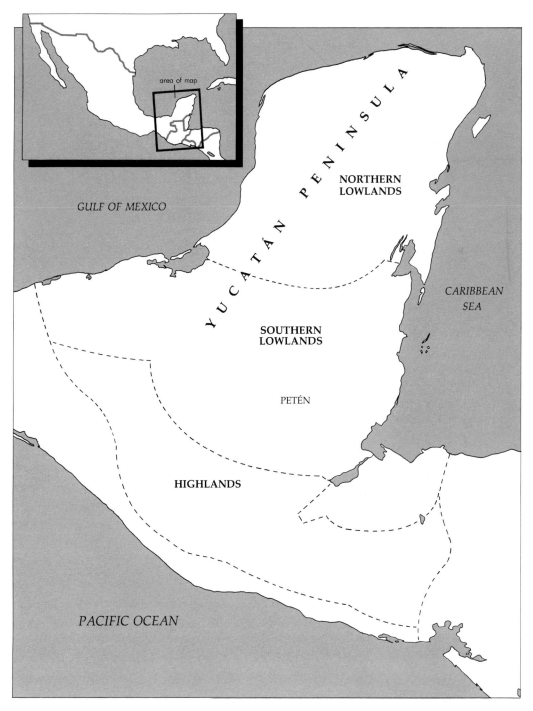

area of map

GULF OF MEXICO

YUCATÁN PENINSULA

NORTHERN
LOWLANDS

CARIBBEAN
SEA

SOUTHERN
LOWLANDS

PETÉN

HIGHLANDS

PACIFIC OCEAN

sion have produced a landscape of deep ravines between hog-back ridges and a few broad valleys, such as the location of Guatemala City. Today, rich southern highland valleys support the largest Maya population. Fertile volcanic soils and a springlike climate have lured settlers there for more than 3,000 years. Yet, earthquakes and volcanic eruptions sometimes belie the rich promise.

The earliest centers of Classic Maya civilization arose in the lowlands, primarily in the area called the Petén. In this heartland, the ancient Maya reached their Classic "golden age" from the 3rd to 9th centuries. In the rain forest lives a wide variety of animal life, including boas, coral snakes, and the deadly pit viper, the fer-de-lance. Spiders, scorpions, and stinging insects, such as wasps, abound. Food animals include deer, turkeys, and rabbits. Ancient Maya raised stingless bees as a source of honey, and their descendants keep hives today. Spider monkeys and small noisy howler monkeys are plentiful. The dangerous jaguar, largest of the world's spotted cats, was hunted by the ancient Maya for its resplendent pelt and was symbolic of power and prestige.

In the northern lowlands, the Yucatán peninsula, a single great limestone shelf juts like a giant thumb up into the blue waters of the Gulf of Mexico. Its eastern shore faces the Caribbean. The peninsula formed over an immense period of time as millions of seashells and corals accumulated. After they were transformed into limestone,

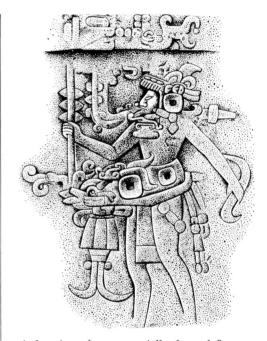

A drawing of a ceremonially dressed figure carved near a cave entrance in Loltun, Yucatán. The art style has Olmec roots, but the work was created after the fall of their civilization.

the landmass rose from the sea. The ancient Maya used limestone as fine building material, easily quarried with stone tools. Limestone forms a hard, durable surface when exposed to the elements. The limestone holds deposits of chert, or flint, which the Maya chipped into tools for cutting and scraping.

Northern Yucatán, in contrast to the southern lowland forest, is low and flat. Lakes are rare and the absence of surface water makes thirst a serious problem. The climate is hot, especially at the close of the dry season. Rains come in

May and last through October. Yucatec animal species are adapted to a dry habitat. The early Maya called Yucatán "the Land of the Turkey and the Deer."

In highlands and lowlands, ancient and modern Maya have depended primarily on food from their cornfields, or *milpas*. For perhaps 4,000 years, the Maya farmer has planted his milpa in the same way. He laboriously fells the trees, burns the brush, and clears the land. Ancient Maya hacked the vines and saplings with stone tools; today, workers use steel machetes. In order to prepare a new field, a farmer selects a patch of forest in a well-drained area. He cuts the trees usually during late autumn, leaving them to dry out until the end of the dry season, when he sets fire to the dead trees and brush. During this season, the sun often seems blackened by smoky haze. After clearing the land, the farmer—with his sack of maize kernels—plants as his forefathers did, pushing the fire-hardened end of a digging stick into the soil and dropping kernels into the hole, sometimes adding bean seeds, whose long vines later curl about the cornstalks. The only change today is that there are metal tips on the sticks. From May to September, he weeds the milpa several times. When the maize ripens, he bends the stalks down below the ears to prevent rain from running into the ears and causing mold. After the kernels have hardened in late fall, the farmer harvests his crop. This process, known as slash-and-burn agriculture, soon exhausts a field. He must shift to a new plot, leaving his old milpa fallow for 4 to 7 years in the Petén and 15 to 20 years in Yucatán. For centuries, Maya planters also turned swamps and floodplains into raised fields by piling up soil between ditches to create fertile plots. In hilly places, they built stone-wall terraces to prevent soil erosion. They also planted small gardens near their houses as they do today.

For centuries, Maya women have fed their families from the maize crop.

A stone sculpture of the Maya maize god that was found in a palace erected in Copán by Yax Pac. The sculpture rose from the head of a stone Cauac monster that ornamented the palace doorway.

After harvest, the woman prepares flat corn cakes using an ancient process that must be done each day. First, she places the dry, shelled corn in a vessel with water and lime to soften the kernels. This mixture is brought almost to the boiling point and allowed to set until the following morning, when she washes the softened corn and discards the hulls. In Classic times, she then ground the kernels into a thick dough (*zacan*) with a mano and metate. Today, she may use a hand-operated mill or go to the village mill. Before the main meal of the day in the early afternoon, she pinches off a lump of dough about the size of a hen's egg, patting it to form a round, thin, flat cake, or *tortilla*, which she bakes on a heated stone griddle. The continuous pat-pat-pat produces a familiar sound echoing throughout all Maya villages about midday. Finally, she places the cake in a gourd to keep it piping hot. Lured by the smell of freshly cooked maize, children often plead for a hot tortilla with a dot of honey on it. Deer, turkey, or duck may be served with the tortillas, when available. Young girls have learned this process from their mothers for centuries. Growing, harvesting, and cooking maize is literally the staff-of-life process for Maya families.

Maya history and civilization have developed through hundreds of generations of maize farmers. Each generation keeps alive the legacy of domestic corn from early Mesoamericans. Corn, more correctly called maize, has always been the Maya's staple crop, compris-ing perhaps 80 percent of their ancient diet. According to the *Popul Vuh*, the flesh of Maya ancestors was made of maize. Many Maya continue to pay homage to the gift of life that reminds them of their sacred origin.

Twentieth-century archaeologists and botanists have sought the origins of domestic maize and other plants through Mesoamerica. Pioneering re-search by archaeologist Richard M. MacNeish and others has established a chronology for the gradual process that probably happened at several sites. The process began 10,000 to 12,000 years ago when early hunters used fluted points termed *Clovis*. A small Clovis projectile point of obsidian found just west of Guatemala City by a picnicking boy is one of the oldest artifacts from Maya country. The end of the Glacial Age changed conditions drastically for the large-game hunters. As the ice receded in high latitudes of North America, temperatures rose and Mesoamerica's large grazing herds of mammoths, mastodons, horses, and giant bison disappeared. Hunting bands preyed on deer, rabbits, and other small game. Actually, they depended on their plant collecting more than their hunting. After about 7000 B.C., the early people embarked on a new stage called Archaic (7000–2000 B.C.) in which efficient collecting and cultivating technology gave rise to the first villages. Continuing to select more productive varieties of corn, beans, and other plants, the people increased their ability to feed expanding populations.

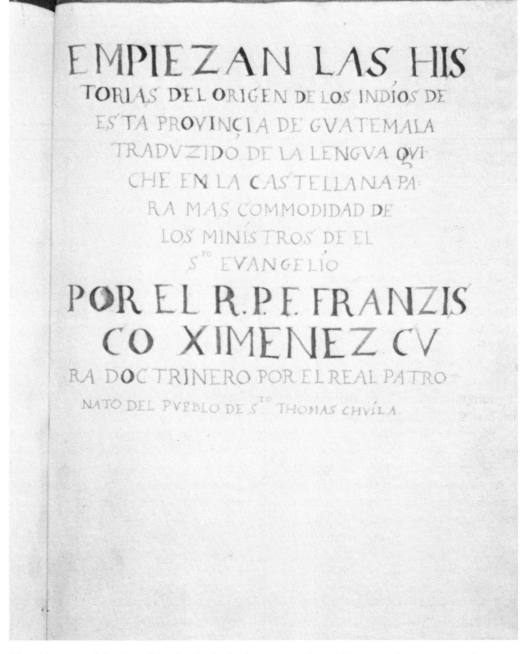

The title page of the Popul Vuh, *the book of Maya myth and history. The writing explains that Father Franzisco Ximenez translated the book from Quiché Maya into Spanish.*

The best evidence for the transition from hunting-and-gathering to settled life and the origin of agriculture comes from the Tehuacán Valley in Mexico. Its extremely dry climate guaranteed perfect preservation of ancient plant remains in caves and rock shelters. MacNeish describes his remarkable discovery: "I scrambled in and out of 38 caves and finally struck pay dirt in the 39th. . . . On February 21, 1960, we dug up six corncobs, three of which looked more primitive and older than any I had seen before." Analysis in a carbon-14 laboratory calculated the specimens' age at 5,600 years. Having arrived at a place where corn had been domesticated, MacNeish and his team excavated the rich site: "Working downward, we found that the cave had 28 separate occupation levels, the earliest of which may date to about 10,000 B.C." The cave's remarkable sequence of human habitation spanning nearly 12,000 years is the longest recorded for any New World area. MacNeish has also excavated in the Maya area of Belize, where he established a tentative sequence from about 7500 to after 2000 B.C. Unfortunately, the preservation of plant remains was poor, but he proved that native people had occupied the lowlands at least 4,000 years ago.

Other archaeologists and scientists seek evidence for the origins of Maya civilization and its development within the region called Mesoamerica. Maya civilization did not develop in a vacuum. Several characteristics of the Mesoamerican people influenced Maya life: sacred calendars, deities, the use of cacao (chocolate) as money and as a ritual beverage, folding-screen books made from bark paper or deerskin, a ritual ball game, pyramidal architecture, and maize cultivation. On the eve of the Formative Period, about 2000 B.C., the early Maya were using stone tools, making pottery and baskets, honoring their dead, and living in villages. During the Formative Period (2000 B.C. to A.D. 250), they established village farming with intensive settlement of the land. By the close of the Formative Period, the Maya were building pyramids, constructing ceremonial centers, and inscribing stone monuments.

Meanwhile, beginning about 1500 B.C., a successful agricultural people, now known as the Olmec, created the first Mesoamerican civilization. The Olmec flourished on the hot, fertile plain of what is now Veracruz, Mexico. This land, with rich levees along sluggish rivers, had attracted farmers for centuries. The Olmec left a legacy that provided a basis for the Mayan development of powerful chiefdoms, carved stone monuments, gods, calendars, and a far-reaching trade network.

San Lorenzo, the oldest Olmec center, was probably a theocratic chiefdom with an elite class and commoners controlled by one political and religious ruler. It flourished between 1200 and 900 B.C., when San Lorenzo lords organized prodigious labor projects. Hundreds of laborers leveled a hilltop, built platforms, and placed monuments on them, the most famous being carved

A jade ax carved with the likeness of a were-jaguar, from the Olmec period. Like the Maya, the Olmec revered the jaguar.

One of several giant stone heads found at the Olmec site of San Lorenzo. The sculptures may represent Olmec kings.

An Olmec quartzite pectoral, which was worn around the neck so that it hung down against the chest (where the pectoral muscles are located). It depicts an Olmec god and signaled that the wearer, probably a king, had a connection with the supernatural.

colossal heads—probably royal portraits. Workers moved 140 million cubic feet of earth, hauling basket after basket of silt to create finger-shaped ridges.

Life in San Lorenzo ended violently in about 700 B.C. In the 1960s, archaeologists excavated stone carvings of human and animal figures that had been ritually "killed" (deliberately mutilated) and then ceremonially buried along the ridges. What mysterious hands smashed sculptures, knocked heads off monuments, and defaced altars 3,000 years ago? Invaders is one guess, but the systematic destruction and burials suggest the Olmec chose the fate of their stone carvings. Scholars are unable to explain these acts.

After the destruction of San Lorenzo, Olmec civilization continued at the La Venta center for approximately 500 years longer. Unique earthworks and stone monuments were built there, and scientists found the La Venta tomb holding two youths who had been wrapped and covered with red paint. Beautiful jade figurines, beads, and offerings had been laid around them, indicating their social status.

Skilled Olmec artists often sculpted jade objects of the were-jaguar, a being with human and jaguar features. Symbolizing power, this giant feline was associated with rain, sky, and lightning. On the oldest dated monument in the New World—31 B.C.—an Olmec sculptor carved a were-jaguar mask on a stone stela with stone tools.

Another important artifact depicting the were-jaguar is a quartzite pectoral that was created by an Olmec artist and then reused by a Maya artist. On the front of the stone, the Olmec artist carved an Olmec god with a human nose and eyes and a jaguar-shaped mouth. Centuries later, a Maya artist incised a ruler's portrait and his accession record on the rear of the plaque. This accession is the earliest historical event to have been deciphered in Maya inscriptions. The ruler is shown wearing jade ornaments tied around his upper arms and wrists, and a heavy jade necklace. The artist carved an owl head adjacent to the portrait to symbolize the ruler's name. This precious green pectoral links Olmec and Maya cultures across many miles and centuries.

Sometime before 100 B.C., Olmec civilization collapsed for unknown reasons. The society depended on a flow of trade goods, and therefore scholars theorize that emerging centers in other areas may have challenged the Olmec's control of lucrative routes. Two later trade centers influenced Maya history: Teotihuacán in the valley of Mexico and Kaminaljuyú in the Guatemalan highlands. Kaminaljuyú was probably powerful enough to resist Olmec domination. Originating as a tiny settlement approximately 3,000 years ago, the Kaminaljuyú chiefdom grew to 20,000 people by A.D. 600. It emerged as a mercantile power at the crossroad for north-south trade routes. Trade in obsidian and raw jadeite generated wealth for a complex society of priests, farmers, artisans, and rulers. Perhaps a ruler commissioned what is now called Stela 11 to commemorate his status. A man wearing an ornate headdress and carrying a fancy knife in his left hand is carved on the granite slab.

The great wealth of Kaminaljuyú's chiefs furnished two spectacular tombs within a huge earthen mound, which were discovered in the 1960s. This royal resting place is the largest of 200 Kaminaljuyú mounds. The tombs' occupants remain nameless, but their rich burials tell of the treatment of the regal dead and the values of those who buried them.

Archaeologists have determined how the great mound was constructed. The mound itself actually consists of six separate structures. Over a long period of time, laborers completed six pyramids, each superimposed over the previous one. (Pyramid 2 completely enclosed pyramid 1, and so on.) Lacking suitable stone, the builders made adobe—a mixture of water, black soil, brown clay, and grass—and added broken pottery fragments to strengthen it. This mixture was applied wet and then tapped firmly in place with a wooden tool. Fragments from approximately 500,000 vessels were used to strengthen this single mound. Replastering must have been an annual event following each rainy season.

Archaeologists have only excavated tombs in pyramids 5 and 6 but suspect the other pyramids also contain burials. For the burial in pyramid 6 (known as Tomb II), Kaminaljuyú workers cut into the top of the pyramid to create a rectangular tomb. The funeral probably began with an impressive procession of family, friends, priests, and civic leaders. The body, richly dressed and painted a brilliant red, was probably extended on a wooden litter and borne slowly through the city, accompanied by sad music from drums and the lamentations of mourners. The open tomb and great pyramid may have been decorated with banners and flowers. When the procession eventually reached the

pyramid, a few elite might have ascended with the body to the summit. At the tomb's edge, they carefully lowered the litter and placed the ruler's head to the south in the center of the burial chamber. Rich furnishings for the afterlife were placed around the body, and gifts and offerings were heaped on the floor and against the tomb walls. Three people were sacrificed and entombed with the body, perhaps to

A diagram of the interior of Tomb II at Kaminaljuyú. The numbered circles represent the placement of grave goods.

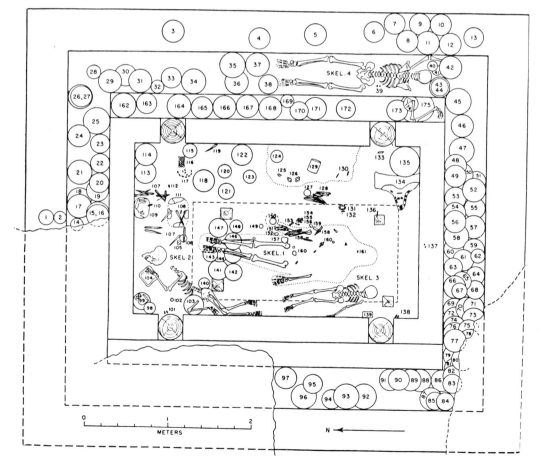

A ceremonial vessel in the shape of a seated man, found at Kaminaljuyú. Its style is associated with Teotihuacán, a center that had a trade relationship with Kaminaljuyú.

attend their master in the next life. Workers laid the roof of wooden cross-beams and covered the tomb with mats. Then they filled the space above the timber roof with earth and laid a new floor flush with the summit platform.

No doubt these somber citizens would have been dismayed had they known that looters would later violate Tomb II and filch jades that covered the ruler's head and chest. Recently, a real estate construction project in Guatemala City destroyed most of the site. Little did the people of Kaminaljuyú realize that its ultimate fate would be destruction by bulldozers.

When the ruler was buried in Tomb II, Kaminaljuyú was flourishing. Its star began to sink about A.D. 200 and the settlement declined until the arrival of traders and perhaps warriors from Teotihuacán brought new wealth and ideas. Whether their appearance was welcome or forced is unknown, but the foreigners and local Maya created a hybrid culture with Mexican-Maya traits. They constructed tombs using the old method, but the contents reflect evidence of Teotihuacán artistic influence. Teotihuacán also influenced other Maya centers throughout the Petén and as far north as Yucatán.

Teotihuacán, a metropolis of perhaps 200,000 people at its zenith, was the cultural, commercial, and religious center of Mesoamerica for 700 years. This first Mesoamerican city had a profound impact on Maya development. Two mighty structures, the Pyramid of the Sun and the Pyramid of the Moon, dominated the prestigious center. Built about A.D. 125, the Pyramid of the Sun was as tall as a 20-story building and supported a temple on its summit. What an awesome sight it must have been with enormous, crownlike ornaments made of wood and straw—covered with bright flowers and fringed with brilliant green quetzal feathers—on the roof. Archaeological evidence suggests that far to the south, Kaminaljuyú was apparently linked to Teotihuacán trade routes. During the early Classic years, Kaminaljuyú engineers constructed small adobe pyramids resembling the Pyramid of the Sun and the Pyramid of the Moon. Teotihuacán's greatness faded about A.D. 700, perhaps from political turmoil and agricultural failure. The city was abandoned and forgotten until centuries later when Aztecs made pilgrimages to its ruins, which they named "the place of the gods."

Like all Mesoamerican centers, Teotihuacán depended on maize for the foundation of its civilization. The development of agriculture was the greatest change in the lives of the Formative Period people, because it made possible villages, then cities, and finally civilization. The key to understanding the rise of Mesoamerican civilizations is maize. Where it flourished, so did elaborate civilizations such as the Olmec, the Aztec, and the Maya. All depended on this staff of life. With the legacy of plant domestication and the origin of village life, all conditions were ready for the rise of the Classic Maya. ▲

A stone panel, dated 783, depicting a Maya lord (top), one of his war captains, and three captives. The scene probably commemorates a successful military expedition. The glyphs (symbols) under the lord indicate that he ruled a lesser center during the reign of Shield Jaguar II of Yaxchilan.

THE RISE
OF THE
CLASSIC MAYA

During the Classic Period, the Maya created one of the most remarkable civilizations in the ancient world. From A.D. 250 to 900, many urban centers of commerce, ceremony, and royal rule flourished in the lowlands of the Petén-Yucatán peninsula. Classic Maya used their incredible skills in mathematics, astronomy, and calendaring to erect monuments, calculate time, and record historical events.

As brilliant mathematicians, the Maya operated a number system with only three symbols: a bar for five, a dot for one, and a shell for zero. This last symbol marked the Maya as great thinkers because, although it may seem unthinkable today, at the time of the early Maya civilization, most of the world's civilizations had no way to symbolize the concept of nothing. The Maya used the shell, the bar, and the dot in different combinations to indicate numbers between 0 and 19. They indicated numbers above 19 by position. In the decimal system (based on the number 10), a person moves 1 position to the left upon reaching 10. The Maya moved 1 position *upward* when they reached 20 in their vigesimal system (based on the number 20). Numbers are written horizontally in the decimal system, whereas the Maya wrote in vertical columns with the lowest values at the bottom and the highest at the top.

Maya priests used mathematics to interpret calendars for marking events in rulers' lives, guiding the agricultural year, determining uses for ceremonials, and recording celestial movements. The ancient Maya inherited from other Mesoamericans three calendars: the Haab, the Tzolkin, and the Calendar Round. The Haab, approximating the solar year, consisted of 18 months of 20 days each. The total of 360 days left 5

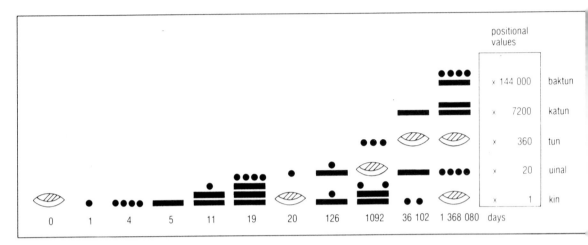

Examples of Maya numerals. A shell symbol denoted zero, a dot stood for one, and a bar represented five.

days known as the *Uayeb*. The Maya considered this time unlucky and dangerous, so they fasted and obeyed sacred rules to avoid evil happenings. At this time, they observed the New Year religious ceremonies.

The Maya consulted the Tzolkin, or sacred almanac of 260 days, to determine ceremonial patterns. Each day's name consisted of a number (1–13) combined with 1 of the 20 day names, for example 13 Ahau. The Maya thought that time was divine and believed that gods carried days on their backs as precious burdens. For example, in the diagram, the god of number 13 unloads Ahau at the end of his day's march. Time was alive for the ancient Maya, who kept close communion with cosmic forces through the sacred count of days. People linked their lives to the lives of the gods. A child's birthday was the day

of the sacred calendar on which he was born and that day's god became his patron deity. Each day carried its own omens and luck. The sacred round of days operated as a wheel of fortune guiding Maya lives. Today, in highland Guatemala, parents still name their children from their birth dates, and the fateful count of days survives under the care of calendar priests, or Daykeepers.

Meshing the 360-day Haab with the 260-day Tzolkin like 2 interlocking cogwheels produced the Maya Calendar Round. For example, 13 Ahau in the Tzolkin coincided with the Haab day 18 Cumcu every 52 years. This combination occurred only once in every 52 years, at which time the cycle of combined dates in the Calendar Round would start over again. This 52-year cycle created the Calendar Round. In addition to using the Tzolkin, the Haab, and the Calendar Round, the Maya refined a fourth method of measuring time—the Long Count.

Scholars calculate the beginning date for the Long Count to be August 13, 3114 B.C., which probably denotes the date that the Maya believe creation occurred. Counting forward from this date, the Maya used 5 cycles: *baktuns* (144,000 days), *katuns* (7,200 days), *tuns* (360 days), *uinals* (20 days), and *kins* (1 day). The Maya wrote these time periods using glyphs. For example, the inscription on the back of the Leyden Plate illustrates how they wrote one date. The first 6 glyphs record that 8 baktuns, 14 katuns, 3 tuns, 1 uinal, and 12 kins have passed since the starting date of 3114 B.C. The next 4 glyphs indicate that this day fell on 1 Eb in the Tzolkin and in the month of Yaxkin in the Haab. Using their own numbers, modern scholars write Maya Long Count dates. They write this date

A diagram of the Maya's interlocking Tzolkin (left) and Haab calendars, which together constituted the Calendar Round. The date represented by the junction of the two calendars is 13 Ahau 18 Cumca.

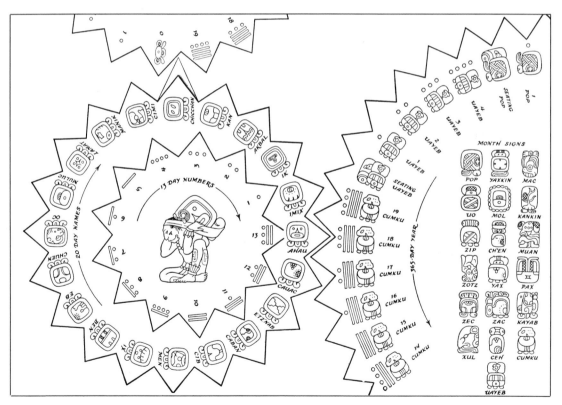

8.14.3.1.12 1 Eb O Yaxkin. In the calendar used in the United States, the date is Friday, September 17, 320. This method of counting time is similar to that used in the United States and other Western nations. For instance, when students write April 26, 1990, they mean that 3 month periods, 26 day periods, 1 thousand-year period, 9 hundred-year periods, 9 ten-year periods, and 0 one-year periods have passed since the beginning of the chronology Americans use.

The Maya recorded their history, including dates, in hieroglyphic writing. Hundreds of hieroglyphic inscriptions appear on wall panels, lintels, stelae, and other monuments. These are primarily dynastic records of births, accessions, victories, and deaths of the elite persons who ruled Classic centers. In 1839 when English explorer and author John Lloyd Stephens examined the Copán inscriptions, he anticipated their content: "I believe that its history is graven on its monuments. . . . Who shall read them?" No one would read them as *historical records* for more than a century.

The decipherment of historical glyphs began in 1958 when Heinrich Berlin proposed that particular glyphs repeated at certain sites were emblem glyphs, which identified a place or its ruling dynasty. At about the same time, Tatiana Proskouriakoff, renowned epigraphist (one who studies inscriptions), proposed that certain inscriptions documented important events in rulers' lives. Following these leads, scholars proved that inscriptions announced the lineage and accomplishments of kings and queens of Copán, Yaxchilan, Tikal, and other great cities. Tikal's Stela 29, dedicated in A.D. 292, is the earliest known lowland monument. Tikal's emblem glyph appears on Stela 29, an emblem that endured for six centuries, illustrating the persistent political power of Tikal throughout the entire Classic Period.

Tikal, one of the greatest and oldest Maya centers, lies in the heart of the Petén jungle in northern Guatemala. Today, its ruins sprawl over many miles. Approximately 3,000 years ago, ancient people settled in this rich rain forest where huge ceiba trees (sacred to the Maya) rose above the lower green foliage to 150 feet. Today, more than 285 species of birds live there, including raucous parrots, golden turkeys, and bright hummingbirds. Large bands of spider monkeys move from tree to tree searching for the fruit of the *ramon* tree. Beyond the Tikal ruins live jaguars, pumas, and ocelots, as well as deer and snakes, including the venomous coral snake. Animal and plant life represented in the art of Tikal indicates that 1,500 years ago the forest appeared much the same as it does today.

Rivers are rare in the region, and for Tikal settlers the most reliable water sources were the water holes called *aguadas*. They constructed 10 artificial reservoirs surrounded by embankments to provide sufficient water during the dry season. The first settlers were probably attracted by the large

MAJOR PRE-COLUMBIAN MAYA SITES

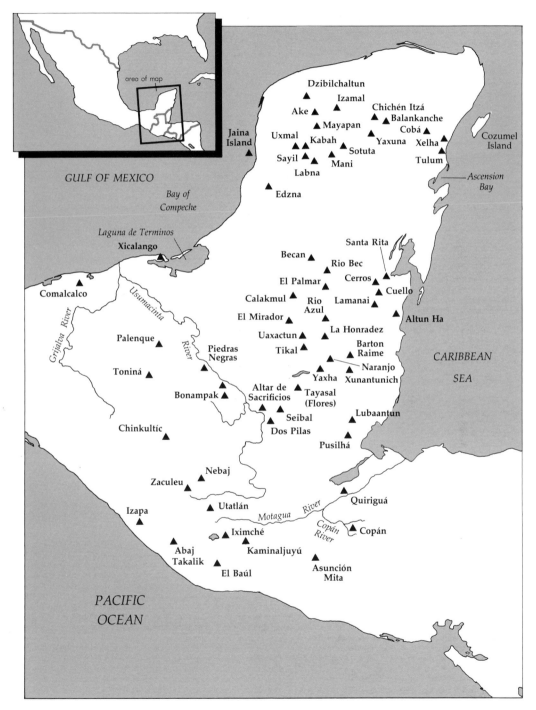

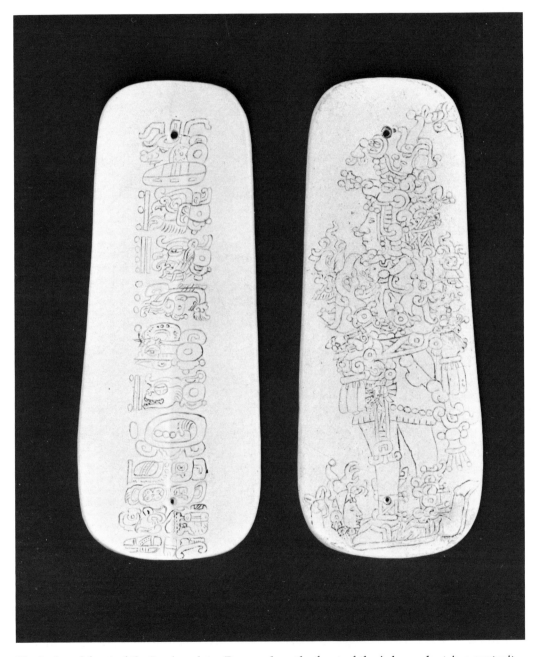

The back and front of the Leyden plate. Engraved on the front of the jade pendant is a portrait of a Maya lord who scholars believe is Jaguar Paw, Tikal's first recorded ruler. The back is inscribed with the Long Count date 320.

supply of flint, valued for making tools, weapons, and trade goods. As early as 700 B.C., they were making flint tools, importing obsidian, and trading in quartzite. In tombs dating about 250 B.C., archaeologists have discovered precious imports: shells and stingray spines from the coasts, and jade and pottery from the Guatemalan highlands. It is clear that Tikal was engaged in an active trade network.

By 100 B.C. Tikal laborers were building massive masonry platforms studded with temples and shrines. Numerous tombs of early rulers have been discovered in the North Acropolis, which occupies 2.5 acres and supports 16 temples. Archaeologists estimate that vestiges of some 100 buildings lie buried beneath the Acropolis platform, the earliest dating back to around 200 B.C.

In 1956, the University of Pennsylvania began a massive archaeological excavation of Tikal ruins. Archaeologists excavated about 6 square miles of central Tikal, revealing over 3,000 structures as varied as lofty temples and pyramids, massive palaces, and tiny households of thatch-roofed huts. They found courts on which the Maya played ball games and a structure in which they took ritual sweatbaths. Concentrated around the ceremonial areas are more than 200 stone monuments, many of them stelae. Maya engineers and artists erected stone monuments at the site for more than 900 years. Archaeologists have also unearthed over 100,000 tools, ceremonial objects, personal ornaments, and other items important in Maya lives. A million-odd potsherds (pottery fragments) have been collected. Archaeologists have used the potsherds to help date the age of Tikal, whose massive scope was the result of probably more than 1,100 years of ceaseless construction.

Such statistics only hint at the enormous richness of Tikal, most of which remains unexcavated. Archaeologists estimate they must work another 100 years to investigate what underlies the mapped surface of central Tikal. The vine-covered, tree-infested temples and palaces have stood silently for almost a millennium.

By A.D. 250, Tikal had eclipsed its rival lowland centers and was flourishing under ambitious kings. Jaguar Paw, Tikal's first ruler, may be portrayed on the Leyden Plate. The carver of the green jade pendant caught the king at the moment of accession, and his royal portrait proclaims his right to rule. Seeing the portrait, ancient Maya recognized that he was sanctioned by the gods, had been victorious in war, and wore the sacred clothes of kings. In the carving, he wears a cloth skirt with a beaded edge. His belt is decorated with crossed-bands, disks, and the Jaguar God of the Underworld. An elaborate loin ornament hangs to his knees, cuffs adorn his wrists, and he wears leather anklets above his royal sandals.

His headdress, adorned with god heads, is also a sign of divine kingship. The main head is a jaguar with nose ornaments. The king holds his arms

The Temple of the Giant Jaguar at Tikal was erected under the orders of King Ah Cacau and served as his burial site.

against his chest—a ceremonial position for holding the double-headed serpent bar, scepter of Maya kings. From the gaping serpent mouths emerge gods sanctifying the king's power: God K on his right and the Sun God on his left. Behind the ruler's feet lies a bound and struggling captive, who will probably be sacrificed. This scene, dated September 17, 320, depicts the earliest known record of a Maya king's accession.

After Jaguar Paw died, Tikal's fortunes continued to be joined to those of the southern Maya, specifically Kaminaljuyú, under a new ruler, Curl Nose, who ruled from 379 to 426. It ap-

pears that the Teotihuacán-Kaminaljuyú alliance involved Tikal as a trading partner. Perhaps Curl Nose was a member of the Kaminaljuyú ruling lineage who came to Tikal and married into the old Jaguar Paw line. In any case, Tikal achieved significant economic success during his reign.

The success of Tikal continued under Stormy Sky, son of Curl Nose, who ruled from 426 to 457. Stormy Sky was the most important of Tikal's Early Classic rulers. During his reign, Tikal extended its acquisition of valuable resources and trade routes, establishing dominance over much of the central lowlands. About 445 he celebrated the end of his first katun in power by erecting the magnificent Stela 31, which portrays himself and places his father, Curl Nose, above his headdress. During his reign, Stormy Sky strengthened the Tikal-Teotihuacán economic and political relationship. Proof of this connection appears on Stela 31. Stormy Sky assumes the traditional Maya pose, but he is dramatically flanked by guards wearing Teotihuacán military helmets and carrying spear throwers, feathered darts, and shields displaying Tlaloc, the Lightning-Hurler Rain God. Other Teotihuacán symbols include the skull on his helmet and the quail on his wrist.

Laden with jade ornaments, Stormy Sky wears the symbols of Maya kingship. In his upraised hand, he displays a string of linked earflares, probably war trophies taken from conquered lords. In the crook of his left arm, he carries a head that displays the Tikal

A sketch of the carvings on Stela 31, a monument erected by Stormy Sky, one of Tikal's great-est kings. He is attended by two guards dressed in the military uniform of Teotihuacán. The image thus celebrates the economic and political relation between Tikal and Teotihuacán.

emblem glyph and traits of the Sun Jaguar God. Like the figure on the Leyden Plate, Stormy Sky wears a royal belt with a Sun Jaguar head at the front and at the back, a jaguar head representing the sun at night. Stormy Sky's name glyph adorns his headdress. (Stormy Sky is, of course, a nickname given him by modern scholars.)

After Stormy Sky's death, Tikal's dynastic history is obscure. Scholars suggest that perhaps many contenders for the throne jostled for power. A ruler named Kan Boar, probably Stormy Sky's son, came to power about 475. Kan Boar's heir, Jaguar Paw Skull, may have ruled from 488 to 537. During his reign, the first woman's portrait appeared on a stela as wife of Jaguar Paw Skull and mother of his successor, Double Bird. During this time, Tikal's economic prosperity and political domination suffered a setback. The number of new constructions and monuments decreased. Simultaneously, Teotihuacán and its sphere of influence began to decline. Long-distance trade through the Maya realm seems to have diminished drastically. Kaminaljuyú connections were broken, and Tikal's control over the southern Maya zone may have disappeared.

Then, Tikal gained new growth after the accession of Ah Cacau in 682. During the Ah Cacau dynasty, Tikal regained its position as primary center of the Petén region. To celebrate his inaugural festivities, Ah Cacau constructed a massive temple that completely covered Stormy Sky's memorial structure. Ah Cacau's subjects removed Stela 31 bearing Stormy Sky's portrait from the foot of its memorial, hauled it up the stairs, and reset it within the rear room of the temple. Then builders filled the interior and literally buried Stormy Sky's physical remains, as well as Stela 31, beneath the largest temple yet built at Tikal. This audacious act signaled Ah Cacau's respect for the past and his initiation of a new era. Ah Cacau reigned 52 years, until 734.

The Temple of the Giant Jaguar—which dominates the east side of the Great Plaza, facing the Temple of the Masks—is a shrine commemorating Ah Cacau's accomplishments and protecting his tomb. It contains an exquisitely carved wooden lintel featuring young Ah Cacau seated on his throne, his feet unable to reach the floor. Behind him stands a giant jaguar protector. On an interior lintel appears an elegantly carved profile of a woman, regally dressed in a *huipil*, a traditional garment, on which an image of God K—the deity of royal lineage—appears. If Ah Cacau built this temple for his wife, this lintel carving may be her portrait.

When archaeologists opened Ah Cacau's tomb in 1960, they found his skeleton adorned with a great jade necklace. He was laid to rest with a treasure-trove—180 pieces of worked jade, pearls, painted ceramics, alabaster, and seashells. One of the more spectacular objects in the tomb was a jade-mosiac miniature portrait of Ah Cacau as a young man. All but the ceramics were expensive imports.

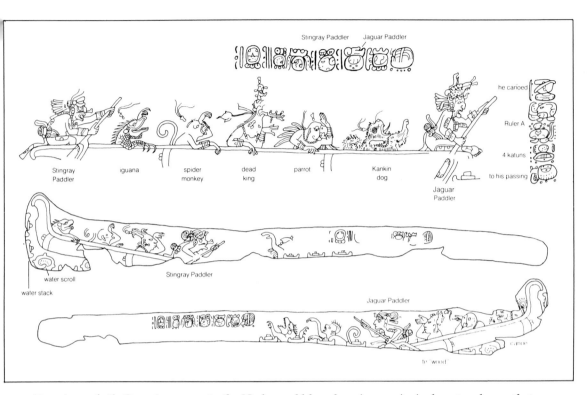

Drawings of Ah Cacau's voyage to the Underworld based on images incised on two bones that were entombed with the ruler. Traveling in a canoe guided by the Old Jaguar God and the Aged Stingray Spine God, Ah Cacau (top center) is accompanied by four animal passengers. The ruler is holding his wrist to his head, a gesture probably indicating that he is dying.

In a corner of Ah Cacau's tomb the scientists found a remarkable bundle of bones. Among the 90 bones, 4 had incised scenes picturing death as a canoe voyage into the watery Underworld. The lowland Maya were a riverine people who transported goods and people in dugout canoes. Therefore, it is not surprising that two of the bones depict a canoe, guided by the Old Jaguar God in front and the Aged Stingray Spine God behind. The canoe carries a dog, a parrot, Ah Cacau, a spider mon-

key, and an iguana. Dated September 16, 775, the text reads, "Ruler Ah Cacau canoed 4 katuns to his passing," meaning that the king lived four katuns until his death.

Under the great Ah Cacau dynasty, which devoted staggering resources to building, Tikal grew to an incomparable Classic city of perhaps 45,000 inhabitants at its zenith. Temple IV, the highest standing aboriginal structure in the Americas, towers 230 feet, and it marks the reign of Ah Cacau's son and successor, Yax Kin. Ah Cacau's grandson, Chitam, constructed twin pyramids and commissioned stelae to record his royal history. He is the last identified Tikal ruler.

By A.D. 869 the last stela had been set in the Great Plaza and construction ceased. Its days of glory gone, Tikal was probably left in neglect by the end of the 10th century. The rain forest claimed the sacred and ancient home of great rulers and their people, and for centuries, the ruins remained unknown to the outside world. In 1848 a Guatemalan government expedition recorded them, but it was not until English explorer and scientist Alfred Maudslay photographed Tikal's architecture and sculpture in 1881–82 that their existence became known to the world at large.

Over several centuries, Tikal expanded, prospered, and declined—a common pattern for Classic Maya centers. Throughout the golden Classic Period, ambitious rulers vied for power and erected monuments whose inscriptions tell the unique history of each center. One of the best-documented royal lineages is the Jaguar dynasty at Yaxchilan, a small center that possibly was under Tikal's domination. Shield Jaguar, the powerful Yaxchilan lord, was a contemporary of Ah Cacau's.

The ancient Maya placed Yaxchilan on the banks of the Usumacinta River, which provided an artery for exchanging ideas and trade goods. Like other Classic centers, it flourished for centuries and then declined. When people left Yaxchilan, a forest canopy sheltered

the buildings and concealed the artistic inscriptions that recorded Yaxchilan's dynastic history. Centuries later, in 1963, epigraphist Tatiana Proskouriakoff made a startling breakthrough. She managed to, in her words, "pry open a chink in the wall of obscurity" when she proved that the silent figures carved into the stone lintels were portraits of Maya royalty who had lived in the 8th

Lintel 24 from a temple erected at Yaxchilan by the ruler Shield Jaguar. It depicts a ceremony in which the king holds a torch above his wife, Lady Xoc, as she draws blood by pulling a thorn-studded rope through a hole in her tongue. Maya nobles regularly gave blood in this manner as a sacrifice to their gods.

century. Rescuing them from obscurity, Proskouriakoff named the Jaguar dynasty according to its name glyphs—a small, round shield with a bird resting on a jaguar head.

Acceding to the throne in 682, the remarkable Shield Jaguar ruled for 50 years and lived to be more than 90 years of age. He may have led the formation of a military alliance among Tikal, Palenque, and other kingdoms, and he extended Yaxchilan's realm by conquering nearby centers. In one of his inscriptions, Shield Jaguar recorded his capture of a neighboring ruler named Ahau. After this feat, Shield Jaguar took the title, Captor of Death, Captor of Ahau.

Shield Jaguar, warrior king and religious leader, recorded three important events on lintels set above the portals of a Yaxchilan temple. The first scene, dated October 28, 709, depicts Shield Jaguar and his wife, Lady Xoc, engaging in a bloodletting ritual. During the ceremony, participants caused themselves to bleed and offered the blood as a tribute to the gods. Shield Jaguar holds a torch-staff above his kneeling wife, who pulls a thorn-studded rope through her tongue. The rope falls into a basket holding a stingray spine (an instrument for drawing blood) and blood-spotted paper.

The costumes depicted in Maya art help explain the actions in each scene and their ceremonial significance. The royal regalia worn by Shield Jaguar and Lady Xoc in the temple carvings were a "text" for the average Maya to read.

In this carving from Lintel 25, Lady Xoc sacrifices as she burns the paper on which her blood has fallen. As the smoke rises, it is transformed into a double-headed serpent. A warrior's head, adorned with a jaguar-skin helmet, emerges from the mouth of one serpent.

Shield Jaguar wears a pleated cape, a Sun God necklace, and elaborate jaguar-skin sandals—symbols of his divine royalty. Jade ornaments encircle his wrists and knees. Lady Xoc also wears royal garments and jewelry—a cape and cuffs of jade or shell mosaic cover her shoulders and wrists. Her elegant huipil is woven in diamond patterns representing the four quarters of the world moving through time; signs for the sky and the planets decorate the end of the garment. Wearing this ceremonial robe, Lady Xoc symbolically stands at the center of the world, where, through her act of bloodletting, she can communicate with supernatural spirits.

In the second lintel carving, Lady Xoc again makes a blood offering. This time, she burns the papers on which her blood has fallen and as the smoke rises from the basket, it is transformed into serpents. A double-headed serpent coils above Lady Xoc and from its mouth emerges a warrior wearing a jaguar-skin helmet. The four-petaled flower design cut out of her garment forms an opening symbolizing the mouth of the earth monster whose jaws receive and release dead souls. In the center of her garment is the braided knot, the glyph for royalty. Lady Xoc wears what she sees—a royal supernatural being emerging from the jaws of the Underworld.

The final lintel scene pictures Shield Jaguar holding a knife and dressed for battle in stone-studded cotton armor. Lady Xoc presents him with his shield and jaguar helmet. Her huipil is similar to the one she wears in the first scene but bears the image of a toad sitting in the center of the diamond design. For the Maya, the toad symbolizes the rain that causes the earth to bloom. Thus, Lady Xoc wears the toad as a symbol of prosperity during Shield Jaguar's reign. As a whole, the three lintel scenes depict common themes in Maya

life: the glory of the ruler, warfare, and personal sacrifice to the gods.

Ancient Maya religiously sacrificed blood. Diego de Landa, first Christian bishop of Yucatán, described this ritual among the Yucatec Maya: "They offered sacrifices of their own blood. . . . They pierced their tongues in a slanting direction from side to side and passed bits of straw through the holes with horrible suffering." The Maya believed bloodletting sanctified rulership and maintained world order, and they offered blood on many occasions: when they dedicated buildings, planted crops, named children, and buried the dead. The lancet, an instrument for drawing blood, was a sacred object to the Maya. The sacrificial paper onto which their blood fell was burned in a brazier to transform the sacred substance into smoke for the gods to consume. As the royal link between gods and humans, King Jaguar and Queen Xoc appear in a bloodletting scene; gods and humans could not exist without each other in Maya cosmology.

Shield Jaguar's successor, his son Bird Jaguar, performed many of the same acts as his father. He erected a series of historical monuments, and his queen performed sacrificial rituals. Like his father, Bird Jaguar had these events recorded in inscriptions. One such scene shows Bird Jaguar and a comrade taking two captives who wear their name glyphs on their thighs. The text states that on May 9, 755, Bird Jaguar seized his most famous captive, Jeweled Skull—a feat that gave him great

A drawing, after a carving on a temple from Yaxchilan, that depicts the ruler Bird Jaguar, his governor, and two captives. Captives taken during battle were subjected to ritual tortures performed to honor the Maya's gods.

prestige. The captives, stripped of battle dress, grovel on the ground. This scene demonstrates that one aim of Classic Maya warfare was to capture prestigious enemies who were then taken back to the city for a series of rituals leading to their death.

In a second scene, dated March 28, 755, Lady Six-Tun, Bird Jaguar's wife, performs her queenly duty of offering blood in order to have a vision. The Maya believed such visions were the embodiment of an ancestor or god. Lady Six-Tun wears a fine huipil of the

During some bloodletting rituals, the Maya sought visions. Lintel 15 shows Lady Six-Tun, a wife of Bird Jaguar's, having a vision of a serpent from whose mouth emerges the head of a human spirit.

same pattern as the one that Lady Xoc wore. Jade jewelry decorates her wrists, ears, hair, and neck. Before her, a serpent rises from a clay bowl lined with bloodied paper, and a human spirit emerges from the rearing serpent's mouth. Lady Six-Tun holds a woven basket and the rope she has used rests across her forearm. Visions, induced by bloodletting, are important ways to commune with gods.

Maya rulers immortalized their names and deeds on stone and wooden monuments, but the common people who supported the centers also left evidence of their lives. Tikal's 45,000 citizens required a host of workers to provide adequate supplies of water, firewood, and food for a single day. Rulers in Tikal, Yaxchilan, and other places mobilized thousands of people to build temples and other structures. Each project required laborers for quarrying and transporting stones; engineers and stone masons for planning and constructing buildings; priests for determining the proper calendric combinations to please the gods; and artists for inscribing the stelae. In the absence of beasts of burden, caravans of human carriers packed goods from one center to the next. Craftsmen fashioned canoes for cargo fleets to serve Yaxchilan and other riverside settlements. Growers, harvesters, thread spinners, and weavers all labored in the widespread cotton industry to produce the simple garments and exquisite fashions to clothe all the Maya. Toolmakers chipped flint and obsidian into incredibly sharp utilitarian and ceremonial blades. A huge work force was constantly preparing walls and thatching roofs for homes.

These tasks were performed endlessly every day of the year, as the early Classic centers rose and fell. Indeed, the daily life of the Maya workers changed very little as Maya civilization progressed through the Classic Period, although elite demands on laborers undoubtedly grew as the centers expanded. The Maya made great advances in mathematics, astronomy, and calendaring, yet all the splendors that signified Classic Maya culture depended entirely on the skill and energy of the hands of its people. ▲

A stucco head from the Temple of Inscriptions, Pacal's tomb at Palenque. The profile emphasizes the long nose and slanted forehead admired by the Classic Maya.

A TIME
OF
SPLENDOR

Around A.D. 600 the lowland Maya Classic world began to recover from the political and economic disruption following the disappearance of the power and influence of Teotihuacán. Several centers exercised dominion over lowland regions. Tikal recovered as the magnet center of the Petén region; Yaxchilan controlled the Usumacinta region; Palenque dominated the southwestern region; and Copán became the primary center in the southeast. These city-states remained independent, but communication and exchange stimulated common cultural patterns that culminated in a golden age of wealth and artistic achievement.

During this time of splendor, warrior kings took captives in hand-to-hand combat for public display. Across the Maya realm, victorious rulers commissioned monuments proclaiming their military prowess. If their royal re-

ports had been written as modern headlines, they might read:

Ah Cacau of Tikal Captures
Smoking Jaguar Paw - 695
Ruler 3 of Tonina Captures Kan-
Xul of Palenque - 709
Shield Jaguar of Yacchilán
Captures Lord Ah-Achuen of
Bonampak - 729
Cauac Sky of Quirigua Captures 18
Rabbit of Copán - 737
Bird Jaguar of Yaxchilan Captures
Jeweled Skull - 755

In 1946, American photographer Giles Healy discovered a dramatic record of this type. In Chiapas, Mexico, Lacandon Indians led him through the rain forest to a Bonampak temple, previously unknown to the rest of the world. The astonished Healy saw paintings covering the walls of three vaulted rooms. The spectacular murals had been preserved by a heavy deposit of limestone formed by constant water seepage for over a thousand years.

In explaining the paintings, scholars theorize that Bonampak artists recorded a splendid pageant of Classic rulership. Under the command of ruler Chaan-Muan, an heir was announced, celebrations held, a battle won, and sacrifices completed. In one scene, King Chaan-Muan and his wife Lady Rabbit, from a royal Yaxchilan family, present their son at court on December 4, 790. White-robed lords salute the heir. Later a celebration honors the young heir on November 15, 791, when Venus rose as the evening star. (The date may have been chosen to assure the heir's being a great warrior, because a certain aspect of Venus was associated with successful war events.) At the celebration, musicians play rattles, drums, turtle shells, and trumpets. This Bonampak band forms part of a great procession that also includes figures, perhaps actors, wearing incredible masks.

A later scene depicts Chaan-Muan and warriors fighting for captives to sanctify the new heir. Again Bonampak lords chose a date when astrological signs indicated that powerful Venus would assist them: August 2, 792. Magnificently dressed warriors fight while musicians blow long war trumpets made of wood or bark. The next scene shifts to a stepped platform in Bonampak where a seated naked figure pleads for his life. Chaan-Muan is clad in a jaguar-skin jacket, and Lady Rab-

bit, standing among the noble spectators, is wearing a white robe. Prisoners taken during the raid have been stripped and tortured, and sit or lie pitifully before Chaan-Muan on the steps of the temple.

The Bonampak paintings depict the elaborate court life led by Maya elite during the 8th century. Even at this small site, more than 200 people participate in the mural rituals. The murals also yield historical information about Maya warfare, and their quality demonstrates that Classic Maya society supported highly skilled artists.

Chaan-Muan commissioned the murals to celebrate the legitimation of his heir. They complement the historical information on Bonampak stelae that tell of his own lineage, accession, and royal sacrifice. The inscription on Stela 2 records that he took office and offered blood. Chaan-Muan identifies his father as White Lizard, and his mother as Lady Knot-Skull. He wears a royal headdress, belt, jewelry, and sandals—signs of divine kingship. His mother and wife, dressed in elaborate headdresses and huipiles, hold bowls of folded paper signifying ritual bloodletting.

Depictions such as these emphasize that some women held high positions in Maya society—they shared power in Classic centers as important partners in establishing dynastic lineages. One of the most perfect Maya stelae, a 12-foot monument dated A.D. 782, portrays a royal Copán woman holding the traditional power symbol—a ceremonial

Ornate Stela H from Copán depicts a woman from the city's royal family. Her headdress bears the image of a Maya Rain God.

serpent bar. Above the woman's finely sculpted face rises a headdress decorated with quetzal feathers and a Rain God mask. She wears a jaguar-skin dress with the shirt drawn into a network of jade beads. On the stela sides, carvings of charming young men, possibly youthful Maize Gods, peer from a mythological serpent's coils. The stela stands on a large vault that held several hundred jade beads and small objects.

Copán, home of this stela, was situated on the Copán River, a tributary of the Motagua River in western Honduras. Farmers settled there about 1000 B.C., and one powerful dynasty ruled Copán for centuries. Great Sun Lord Quetzal Macaw founded the dynasty early in the 5th century. Copán's unique Altar Q presents the portraits of 16 rulers, each in royal regalia and seated upon his name glyph. Little is known about the 11 rulers before Smoke Imix, the long-lived king who led Copán through its first great period, 628–695. After Smoke Imix, 18 Rabbit ruled Copán between 695 and 738. As a warrior-king, 18 Rabbit led Copán to one of its most disastrous days—May 3, 738. Inscriptions carved on sandstone Stela E at Quiriguá reveal that its king, Cauac Sky, captured 18 Rabbit and had him beheaded on that date. Quiriguá, ruled by a rival lineage, was only 30 miles north of Copán.

The next Copán ruler, Smoke Monkey, appears to have been a caretaker king from 738 to 749. His son, Smoke Shell, who took the throne in 749, launched construction of the great Hi-

continued on page 53

THE MURALS OF BONAMPAK

Decorating the walls of three rooms in a small temple in Chiapas, Mexico, are the best-preserved paintings made by the Classic Maya. Archaeologists now refer to the ancient city where the temple was located as Bonampak.

The murals at Bonampak depict events that occurred during the reign of King Chaan-Muan in the 8th century. Perhaps more effectively than any other works of Maya art, the paintings communicate the rich pageantry associated with the Maya ruling elite. On the next two pages are portions of painted copies of the Bonampak murals. They show that, although the images certainly have meanings unknown to the modern viewer, the power of these ancient works still survives today.

A Public Sacrifice

At the north end of room 2 of the temple appears a sacrifice of war captives overseen by Chaan-Muan. The event takes place on a temple staircase, where public sacrifices were often conducted.

This detail shows nine figures situated on two stairs. The two captives sitting on the lower stair have been tortured by having their fingernails removed. The captive in the lower right-hand corner rubs his fingers together, possibly in dread of falling victim to the same torture. The figure lying between them has already been killed. A large cut in his chest suggests that his heart has been torn out. Often non-Maya viewers have thought the smooth, flowing outline of this captive was out of place in the gruesome scene. But to the Maya, the grace of the figure might have represented the beauty of the passage from life to death.

On the center of the upper stair, a captive is shown begging for his life. He looks pleadingly into the eyes of Chaan-Muan, who stands to the right, holding a staff. Chaan-Muan does not return the captive's stare but instead looks at the captains standing behind him. Each captain holds a torch and wears an elaborate headdress topped by the head of an animal. The captain closest to the begging captive wears a cape made from a full jaguar pelt and holds his hand out to the ruler. He is pinching his fingers together like the victims, but his gesture probably means that he is offering the most recent victim to his ruler.

A Royal Procession

A mural in room 1 depicts the celebration held when a child of the royal dynasty was presented to the court. Among the participants is a group of six figures in unusual costumes.

On the left in the grouping are two men in reptilian masks. One is handing an ear of maize to the other. Seated in front of them is possibly the leader of the group. Holding his hand in a gesture that might mean he is giving directions to the others, he is the only figure whose own face is visible. Also seated is a man in a crocodile mask. The Maya knew ways of preserving animal parts, so this mask might be the hollowed head of an actual crocodile. The figure above him wears a lobster mask, complete with antennae and gloves shaped like huge lobster claws. To his right stands another masked figure with a huge eye and prominent beard.

continued from page 49

eroglyphic Stairway leading to the summit of a temple. More than 1,250 hieroglyphs carved on the stairway steps chronicle Copán's dynastic history to 755, the longest known Mesoamerican inscription. Unfortunately, the stairway collapsed in the 1800s, leaving beautifully carved fragments scattered on the plaza below, like stone pieces of a giant jigsaw puzzle. Yax Pac, who succeeded to the throne in 763, continued Smoke Shell's construction renaissance and commissioned Altar Q. Highly skilled sculptors carved four Co-

pán kings on each of the four sides. On one side the dynasty founder Quetzal Macaw presents Yax Pac with the sacred insignia of kingship.

Copán's splendid sculpture and architecture remained unknown to the outside world until 1841, when American diplomat John Lloyd Stephens and English artist/architect Frederick Catherwood published *Incidents of Travel in Central America, Chiapas, and Yucatán.* Stephens and Catherwood spent the fall of 1839 to early spring of 1840 at the ruins of Copán, excavating, taking

Frederick Catherwood, John Lloyd Stephens, and their Maya assistants at the site of Tulum on the Yucatán coast, depicted in a late-19th-century lithograph based on a sketch by Catherwood. The two explorers are shown holding a measuring tape in front of the temple.

notes, and sketching its temples and monuments. In order to work undisturbed, Stephens bought the ruins from a local farmer. He wrote: "I paid fifty dollars for Copán. There was never any difficulty about the price. I offered that sum, for which Don José Maria thought me only a fool; if I had offered more, he would probably have considered me something worse." Stephens and Catherwood's book intrigued Alfred Percival Maudslay, noted English archaeologist, who visited Copán in 1881 to photograph prominent monuments. He printed his Copán collection in *Biológica Central Americana*, enabling modern scholars to compare his early visual records with the Copán ruins today.

From the silent ruins of Copán, Tikal, Bonampak, and other cities, scholars recover recorded names and events by deciphering hieroglyphs and decoding ritual scenes. Smoke Imix, Ah Cacau, and Chaan-Muan recorded historical moments on their monuments. For Maya rulers, the cosmos was the origin of supernatural power, and their pictures portrayed royalty's place within that cosmos. In order to read their records, therefore, scholars must understand Maya cosmology—their belief in gods, sacred objects, and sacred symbols in relation to the royal power process.

During the Formative Period, the Maya probably practiced simple nature worship. By the Classic Period, however, an extremely complex religious system guided their daily lives. The universe of the Classic Maya had an Upperworld, Middleworld, and Underworld. The Sun marked the Upperworld in his passage across the sky. The behavior of the Sun and other celestial gods could be either beneficial or dangerous, so Maya priests tracked the movements of the sun, moon, and other planets. The Middleworld was oriented by four directions, each associated with a special bird, tree, and color. At the center of the universe stood the sacred ceiba tree with a divine bird at its crown. The tree joined the three worlds: Its roots stretched down into the Underworld; its trunk spanned the Middleworld; and its branches reached into the Upperworld. The souls of the dead traveled from level to level via this tree.

The foundation of the Maya pantheon was Itzamna, often pictured as a two-headed sky serpent. The ceremonial bar, which rulers hold in their portraits, represents the Lord of the Heavens, Itzamna. Inventor of learning and writing, Itzamna was balanced by his wife, Ix Chel, or Lady Rainbow, goddess of weaving, medicine, and childbirth. All other gods were the offspring of this couple.

God K, also associated with royal power, often forms the scepter that kings clasp on accession, bloodletting, and sacrificial occasions. Rulers frequently used God K's portrait glyph in their names as part of the heraldry of their lineage.

Kings also wore the image of the powerful Sun God. This god had two aspects: Kinich Ahau was the title of the

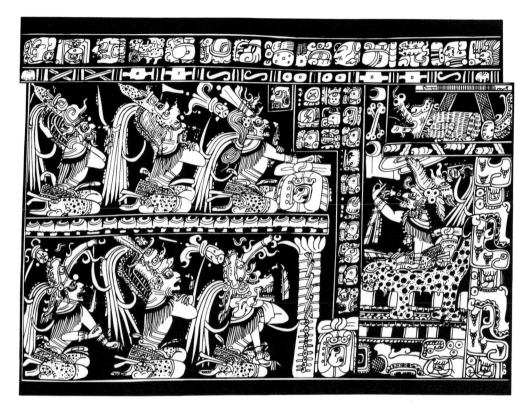

A drawing, based on the Vase of the Seven Gods, showing the God of the Underworld attended by six of his lords. The Maya called their Underworld Xibalba.

day sun as he journeyed across the sky. At sunset the Sun God passed on his night journey beneath the earth into the dark Underworld and became the fearful Jaguar God. This Jaguar Sun appears on warrior shields as patron of war. To identify with the Sun, rulers used Sun titles: Ah Kin, meaning He of the Sun, and Ahau-Kin, meaning Lord Sun. (Ahau means king or great lord; kin means sun or day.)

The Maya also revered Chacs, or Rain Gods, critical deities for maize farmers. Chacs had reptilian faces, down-curling snouts, and twin fangs. Set at the four sides of the world, Rain Gods created lightning and hurled stone axes as thunderbolts. The Maya depicted their Maize God, Yum Kaax, as a handsome youth with maize leaves and an ear of corn sprouting from his head.

Many gods of death dwelled in the Underworld. The souls of dead Maya entered the Underworld, called Xibalba, through a cave or body of water. It is known how the Maya pictured the dreaded Xibalba from paintings on funeral ceramics created to accompany royal souls on their Underworld journey. One death deity, Yum Cimil, had an ugly bloated body, skeletal face, and thin limbs. Death Gods and other Xibalbans are pictured wearing ornaments made of disembodied eyes filched from the dead and dying. One pot depicts God K in his Underworld palace with six Xibalban lords facing him, including the Jaguar Sun.

The Classic Maya believed that all souls went to this "place of fright." According to a story in the *Popul Vuh*, however, after the miraculous Hero Twins defeated the Lords of Death, souls were not trapped there.

Hunter and Jaguar Deer were great ball players, blowgunners, and tricksters. One day while the Hero Twins were playing ball, the Lords of Xibalba became outraged: "They're just stamping around, shaking the earth above us without respect." So the Death Lords challenged Hunter and Jaguar Deer. "Come to Xibalba and play ball with us. Bring your rings, gloves, and face masks. We will turn you into bones and skulls." Accepting the challenge, the twins traveled down Trembling Canyon, past the River of Blood and the River of Scorpions, to four crossroads. "Follow me to Xibalba," said the Black Road. Serpents of laughter multiplied in the hearts of the Death Lords. Upon reaching Xibalba the twins exclaimed: "Hail to 1 Death; Hail to 7 Death; Hail to Skull Staff and Bloody Claws. We have come to defeat you."

The Death Gods rolled a bright ball toward the twins. Shattered bones and a white knife clanged inside as it twisted along the court, but the knife could not slice the twins. "Throw them into the Shivering House, the House of Cold." Fierce was the frost in the home of cold, but the twins made a fire from old logs. "Ah, lock them in the Jaguar House where jaguars are tangled together in a rage." But the twins dumped bones before the beasts, and they warred over the bones. "Now the jaguars are eating their hearts," jeered the Death Lords. But when dawn came, the twins walked free. "You must enter the House of Killer Bats. A house full of Death Bats, huge beasts." Like knives were their fangs, but the twins crept inside their hollow blowguns and were not bitten. "Screech, Screech," all night the bats shrieked, and when Hunter peered out of the blowgun at dawn, a Death Bat snatched his head. His body remained wedged in, headless, and when Hunter's head rolled across the court, all Xibalba rejoiced. Nonetheless, Jaguar Deer cried, "Kick the head as a ball." Jaguar Deer put a pumpkin head on the court; the pumpkin burst and splattered, and again the twins tricked the Lords.

The twins entertained the Dark Lords. Making a great bonfire, 1 Death dared them to leap into the flames, saying, "You shall die." Holding hands, the twins jumped headlong into the fire, but the handsome boys reappeared again, and the Lords were astounded.

A painting on a Maya vase showing one of the Hero Twins dancing and preparing to sacrifice his brother in the Underworld.

"Sacrifice yourselves. We are delighted with your dance." So Jaguar Deer sacrificed Hunter. His legs, his arms, his head came off. His heart was ripped out, and Jaguar Deer went on dancing. "Rise thou again," he said, and suddenly Hunter revived.

Then the Lords' hearts filled with desire and despair over the dancing of the young men. "Do it to us. Sacrifice us," begged 1 Death and 7 Death. "Very well, you will revive. Are you not Death? We dance to delight you." First, they sacrificed 1 Death, and then 7 Death. But they did not revive the horrible Lords. Having killed Death, Hunter and Jaguar Deer walked into the sky; one became the moon (or Venus) and one the sun.

The miracle of the Hero Twins set the sacred pattern for achieving Maya afterlife. Symbols of their miracle appear on tombs and in other special places. One of the most exquisite examples was discovered at the Classic Maya city of Palenque.

The Maya built Palenque in a dramatic place—in hills overlooking a vast forest-covered plain. Plentiful fruit and fish, as well as brilliant blooming flowers, must have made it a pleasant place to live. Palencanos painted temples and pyramids a gleaming red and decorated them with bright stucco designs up to their very roof combs. The city sat like a jewel in the tropical green Chiapas highlands.

Lord Shield Pacal led Palenque to greatness from 615 to 683. The most impressive memorial to a single person in ancient America, the Temple of Inscriptions, honors him. Long before Pacal's

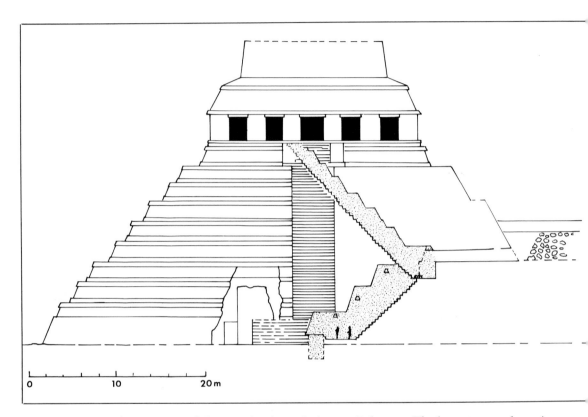

A diagram of the interior of the Temple of Inscriptions at Palenque. The largest mausoleum in Mesoamerica, the structure served as the final resting place of Lord Pacal. After the king's remains were placed in the chamber deep inside the interior of the tomb, the stairway was filled in with rubble.

death, Palenque laborers hollowed the heart out of a single gigantic stone destined to hold his royal body and shaped a great lid from another stone. The entire sarcophagus weighed about 25 tons. The temple holds Pacal's sepulcher and dominates the city.

Hundreds of workers quarried stone blocks from nearby mountains and transported them to the building site. There masons fitted and finished the blocks to create a chamber around the coffin and an enormous pyramid-temple above the tomb. On great stone panels embedded in the walls, artists inscribed 617 glyphs, the longest intact Maya hieroglyphic inscription. It records Pacal's history, including details of his birth, accession, and death, along with the name of his successor, Chan Bahlum.

When Pacal's subjects closed his tomb, they believed they had done so for eternity. But in 1952, almost 1,300 years later, Alberto Ruz broke its seal. Ruz and his workers labored for months removing the rubble that Pacal's people had used to block the staircase leading down to the tomb. Reaching the last step, 65 feet below the temple floor, Ruz recorded, "We had arrived at the door of mystery. Widening the opening slightly, I put the electric light through. . . . To my amazement, out of the shadow arose a vision from a fairy tale." Ruz beheld an enormous room with glistening walls that seemed to be carved from ice. Around them marched tall sculpted figures, like giant guards. The cream-colored coffin filled most of the room; on its lid ancient Palenque sculptors had carved a representation of the Maya universe: Upperworld, Middleworld, and Underworld. The scene depicts the belief system whereby a king dies and a god is born.

The sculpture shows Pacal at the instant of death falling into the Underworld. Like the Hero Twins in the *Popul Vuh*, he will defeat the Lords of Death and ascend to the Upperworld. Pacal's passage into the Underworld is linked to the cosmic movement of the sun. Like the Lord Sun, Pacal will enter the Underworld and emerge as a god. Plunging into the Underworld, the Sun will carry the dead king from the world of the living beyond two huge skeleton dragons forming a U-shaped entrance to Xibalba. Their rising snouts curve inward like a vise holding his body, and between them, the Earth Monster also holds Pacal.

A sketch of the lid of Pacal's sarcophagus from the Temple of Inscriptions. Between 615 and 683, Pacal made Palenque a great political and economic center of the Maya world. The carving depicts the king at the moment of death as he falls from the world of the living into the Underworld. From there, the ruler will be reborn as a god and ascend into the heavens.

Behind Pacal rises the sacred ceiba tree in the shape of a cross. (This plant may also represent a maize stalk.) Undulating over the tree's branches is a double-headed serpent bar from whose wide open jaws emerge God K and the Jester God, symbols of Maya kingship. Jade beads adorn the serpent's mouths and body, a living symbol of the Middleworld, home of the Maya people. Perched atop the tree is the divine bird of the heavens with a God K head. The scene is framed by celestial signs including sun, moon, and Venus. On the sarcophagus sides, sculptors portrayed Pacal's ancestors, including two queens of Palenque: Lady Zac, his mother, and Lady Kan-Ik (Maize Wind), his grandmother, who ruled for 21 years and died in 604.

When Ruz raised the coffin lid, he discovered that the ancient Maya had entombed their lord with pomp and ceremony. Attendants carried the deceased up the steep staircase of the Temple of Inscriptions and down its interior stairway to the sacred crypt. Resting their precious burden carefully in the coffin, they placed a jade bead in Pacal's mouth, a bead in each hand, and a magnificent jade figurine at his feet. Pacal also wore royal jade jewelry: necklaces, bracelets, and rings. A priest covered Pacal's face with a jade mosaic mask with eyes of inlaid pearl—a fitting face for eternity. Attendants wrapped the body in a red cotton shroud and covered the sarcophagus interior with red cinnabar, color of the east where the

sun is reborn each morning. Carefully they lowered the gigantic lid in place. On the floor they placed two superb stucco heads along with vessels containing food and drink.

After the burial rites were completed and the chamber sealed, five or six sacrificial victims were placed in front of the doorway. Later workers laid a hollow tube reaching along the hidden stairway up to the temple floor. Through this conduit, the King-Priest could maintain contact with his subjects, receiving their prayers, continuing to safeguard them with divine power, and transmitting to them the commands of the gods. Finally, laborers filled the long stairway with rubble to conceal their royal secret.

Pacal's son and successor, Chan Bahlum, celebrated his accession by building three exquisite temples and enshrining within each a scene using the same symbols that Pacal used to express divine kingship. One scene located in the Temple of the Foliated Cross, which unites the life cycles of humans and maize with the gods, shows the transfer of power from Pacal to Chan Bahlum. The deceased Pacal stands on a corn plant issuing from a god in a seashell, and the corn leaves wrap around a Maya head. Chan Bahlum stands on a Cauac monster, a figure associated with storm and rain. Both rulers flank a cross motif—similar to the one on Pacal's sarcophagus lid—that rises from the head of the Earth Monster. Sun God profiles project from each

Lady Kan-Ik, grandmother of Pacal, in a sketch based on a carving on Pacal's sarcophagus.

A drawing of a panel in the Temple of the Foliated Cross depicting the transfer of power from Pacal (right) to Chan Bahlum.

side of the cross. Corn plants emerging from their foreheads form the cross arms, on which the heads of young Maya sit in place of ears of corn. This imagery expresses the life cycle and the mythic origin of humans from maize, and underscores the continuity of leadership of this major Classic city through 90 years.

Historical and cosmological information on the Temple of Inscriptions and the temples of Chan Bahlum indicate that Pacal's reign was a pivotal point in Palenque's dynastic history, and subsequent rulers wished to be identified with his power. Five months after Chan Bahlum's death, his younger brother, Kan-Xul, took office and reigned until his capture in 711. Pacal's third son, Xoc, took the throne in 720. By 764 when Kuk became ruler, Palenque's power seemed to have waned. Historical records at Palenque end in 799 with the accession of 6 Cimi Pacal. The later fate of Palenque and its ruling dynasty are unknown.

The fate of other Classic centers also remains a mystery. For centuries, the Maya performed activities supporting the Classic system: planting and harvesting maize, marrying and rearing children, building monuments and conducting ceremonies using precious commodities imported from distant sources. Then cracks appeared in the system and within the 9th century monumental building ceased, population decreased dramatically, trade declined, and Tikal, Copán, Palenque, and other southern and central centers suffered severe calamities. Scant evidence of their demise appears in the final Long Count dates carved in the centers: at Palenque 799; at Bonampak 800; at Tikal 869; at Toniná 909.

Many questions remain unanswered as to why centers declined. Scholars have no conclusive answers, but they have advanced several theories. Probably a number of pressures from within and without the Maya society contributed to its decline. Abuses of power by the elite may have undermined their ability to control political alliances and trade networks, as well as their own subjects. An increasing population demanded more food production. As productivity decreased owing to misuse of land, malnutrition and disease probably increased. Accelerated warfare weakened the city-states, perhaps opening the way for foreign Mexicans to invade and conquer the lowlands.

Classic life-style declined, but Maya civilization did not disappear. It simply moved to another stage with new actors—a smaller populace with different ideas, art, and artifacts for future outsiders to puzzle and ponder over. For a thousand years, the special relationships between kings, gods, and commoners created a Classic age that was destined to rise, flourish, and fall. In the Postclassic era, new mercantile centers would create a culture destined to prosper before suffering the ravages of Spanish conquest. ▲

A section of a panel depicting a ballplayer preparing to receive a ball. It is one of two sections that portray two Maya lords reenacting a scene from the Hero Twins myth. This lord is dressed as the Jaguar God, and the player on the missing panel wears the garments of a lord of the Underworld.

4

THE COUNT
OF
KATUNS

The close of the Classic Period brought dramatic changes in Maya history. The axis of change shifted from the southern lowlands to the northern Yucatán peninsula and the southern highlands of Guatemala. From 900 to 1500 the Postclassic Maya survived conflict and conquest, as they coped with upheavals reverberating throughout Mesoamerica. Long-distance traders developed new Yucatecan power centers that relied on militarism and met Mexican intruders. What may have begun as a clash of cultures ended in a blending of two cultures, for the Maya absorbed the Toltec-Mexican elements and shaped them into one unique Maya culture. Consequently, Chichén Itzá, Mayapan, and other Yucatecan centers contrasted sharply with Tikal, Palenque, and other lowland Classic centers in art, architecture, and political-religious structure.

Postclassic Maya used their legacy of literacy, and modern scholars are deciphering their inscriptions. They are also translating several katun histories called the *Books of Chilam Balam*, three Maya codices, and other sources that give glimpses of Postclassic life. Only a handful of native manuscripts survived the Spanish conquest. One, the *Dresden Codex*, is probably a 12th-century copy of an earlier Classic book.

Compiled and used by Maya priests for divinatory purposes, the codex contains 39 pages of prophecies, ceremonies for the new year, and charts of solar eclipses and planetary movements. Five pages contain a Venus almanac filled with tabulations for priests to consult. The Maya particularly feared times when Venus first appeared as Morning Star because they perceived the rays of Venus to be a god's spears. One page vividly portrays this danger. At the top, the Maize God, holding a vase, confronts a deity seated on a throne, wearing a skull headdress, and death-eye collars. In the middle, an aggressive form of Venus holds a spear thrower and brandishes down-pointed spears that symbolize the planet's death-dealing shafts of light. At the bottom, Venus's victim, a youthful figure, sprawls on the ground, pierced by a spear.

After extensively studying the *Dresden Codex*, Maya scholar J. E. S. Thompson concluded that the Venus almanac predicts a time of peril with drought, hot sun, and no crops. "Woe to the milpa. Woe to the land. Woe to the sea. Woe to the Maize God. Woe to mankind."

The Yucatec Maya also continued the legacy of calendaring, but they favored the Short Count (a cycle of 13 katuns, approximately 256 years), rather than the Long Count, for recording their prophetic histories. In this system, each katun bore the number and name of the day on which it ended, which was always Ahau. Thus the period ending in A.D. 1204 was Katun 8 Ahau. The Maya perceived Katun 8 Ahau as a time of fighting and political change. At every repetition of Katun 8 Ahau, therefore, the Maya expected such calamities to recur.

Like the Classic people, later Maya anchored their life in time inasmuch as the count of katuns controlled their

A mural painting from Chichén Itzá depicting the activities of everyday life in a Maya village.

daily existence. With profound faith that correct calendrical calculations enabled them to predict the fate of the next cycle, priests recorded the events of each katun. The Balam, ruling lord of the katun, announced the predictions at his inauguration. He, or his Spokesman-Chilam, wrote the history of the katun after leaving office as a basis for future prophecy. Thus, the *Books of Chilam Balam* are called prophetic histories.

According to these chronicles, foreigners traveling by sea reached Yucatán during the 10th century. One group, known as Putun Maya, had already developed a trade empire in what are now the Mexican states of Tabasco and Campeche. They were not a unified nation but were many independent groups. These sea traders had probably moved into the central and southern Maya lowlands during the terminal Classic, winning temporary control of Yaxchilan and possibly other centers. Successful warriors and merchants, the Putun may have seized control of trade routes formerly controlled by Classic powers. The lucrative salt trade was a prime target. Cacao, cotton cloth, obsidian, shell, jadeite, slaves, honey, feathers, and a large variety of food products also flowed along trade routes. At the time of the Spanish conquest, the Putun homeland was known as "the land of the canoes."

The Itza (Water Witches), a branch of the Putun, sailed around Yucatán to Cozumel Island and penetrated inland by 918. They renamed the ancient inland site Chichén Itzá or "the mouth of the well of the Itza." These aggressive sailors dominated the trade around the peninsula that connected the east coast and west coast ports. Putun expansion peaked between 918 and 987. Yucatecan chronicles relate that a Putun group, possibly allied with Toltec elite warriors from Tula in central Mexico, eventually established their capital at Chichén Itzá.

These mobile, marginal Maya had already acquired Mexican traits. Living along the extreme western edges of Classic Maya civilization in the Gulf Coast country of Tabasco, they traded and intermarried with their Mexican neighbors, and by the end of the 8th century they adopted Toltec ways. This aggressive group naturally spread Mexican ideologies as they canoed their way up the inland waterways and circled the Yucatán peninsula. The exact nature of the Toltec-Putun relationship remains a mystery, but Mexican and Maya elements exist side-by-side at Chichén Itzá. Scholars grant a long, if controversial, history to the blending of these two cultures.

The mystery involves the Toltec city of Tula (located about 50 miles north of present-day Mexico City) and the legend of the feathered serpent god, Quetzalcoatl. The Toltec settled Tula after the collapse of Teotihuacán. Tula's ruler and high priest, known as Topiltzin, also took the title of Quetzalcoatl or Feathered Serpent because he had served as a high priest to the god before his accession. Native records attribute to him all that is good and great. In the Toltec golden age, Quetzalcoatl

A late-19th-century photograph of a Maya man posing next to one of two columns located at the entryway of the Temple of the Warriors at Chichén Itzá. The sculpture represents Quetzal-coatl, a deity brought to the Maya homeland by the Toltec from the Valley of Mexico.

lived in multicolored palaces, erected great temples, and devoted his life to meditation. Reportedly, Quetzalcoatl's enemy, the Tezcatipoca, bewitched, ruined, and drove Quetzalcoatl from Tula. He fled to the east and, arriving at the edge of the waters, disappeared. According to one account, he cast himself into a great fire, and from the flames his heart emerged as Venus, the morning star. According to another account, he sailed east on a raft of serpents. (The story of Quetzalcoatl, the culture hero and the god, is also told by the Yucatec Maya and the Quiché Maya with the names of Kukulcan and Gucumatz.)

If the serpent raft legend has some factual basis, then Quetzalcoatl would have landed on the Yucatán coast. Maya chronicles tell of the arrival of a man named Quetzalcoatl, translated into Maya as Kukulcan (kuku, "feathered," and can, "serpent"), in a Katun 4 Ahau that ended in A.D. 987. Spanish bishop Diego de Landa states: "They say he was favorably disposed . . . and after his return he was regarded in Mexico as one of their gods and called Quetzalcoatl; and they also considered him a god in Yucatan on account of his being a just statesman."

Whether the Quetzalcoatl arrival story is fact or legend, scholars believe that Toltec invaders introduced the worship of Quetzalcoatl-Kukulcan to the Yucatec Maya, transforming their culture with aspects of Toltec religion, architecture, and social organization. Everywhere on monumental buildings appears the feathered snake, its plumed body terminating at one end in a great head with open jaws ready to strike, and at the other end the warning rattles of the rattlesnake. With these new religious images came signs of Toltec militarism. Images of warriors, jaguars, and serpents abound. In sculpted and painted scenes, lines of proud warriors face an altar where sacrifices were made to the feathered serpent god. In the center of Toltec Chichén stands the Castillo, a great temple-pyramid dedicated to Kukulcan. Inside the Castillo rests a stone throne in the form of a snarling jaguar, painted red, with jade eyes and shell fangs.

At Chichén Itzá the Toltec-Maya built an orderly capital city in which they conducted government affairs, held ritual ball games, and celebrated their military power. Rulers surrounded themselves with symbols of war and sacrifice. Warriors with Toltec titles, such as Jaguar knights and Eagle knights, provided sacrificial prisoners, and priests offered human hearts to the rising sun. Monumental buildings serve as visual records of conqueror and conquered. For example, the Temple of the Warriors was a splendid building surrounded by colonnaded halls. Entering the temple, which may have been the seat of government, citizens passed through rows of square columns carved with Toltec officers bearing weapons and women bearing offerings. People entering the temple would have felt both the comfort of the offering bearers and the threat of the warriors. The entryway to the temple was

The Temple of the Warriors, centerpiece of the Toltec-Maya city of Chichén Itzá. Such huge and impressive monuments affirmed the power and right to rule of the city's leaders.

flanked by towering feathered serpent columns. The great heads, with wide-flung jaws, lie flat upon the floor of the building. The open mouths, painted brilliant red, were studded with fangs in the lower and upper jaws. The eyes were deep-sunken cavities filled in with black paste around yellow-white pupils. Long graceful plumes of bright green feathers were carved upon the shafts of the columns. This was the mystical Plumed Serpent, patron god of Chichén Itzá.

Today, at the top of the stairs a stone *chacmool* stares out upon the main plaza. Chacmools were sculpted hu-man figures lying on their backs with knees and head raised, and their hands holding a bowl-shaped receptacle to receive offerings, perhaps human hearts. In the rear of the temple chamber a great platform supported by miniature Toltec warriors served as the ruler's throne. All interior walls were painted with lively scenes, many relating to the Toltec conquest of Yucatán.

Across the plaza from the Temple of the Warriors stands the Great Ball Court, the largest and finest in Meso-america. Its playing area is about the size of a modern football field. For more than 4,000 years, Mesoamerican people

A chacmool *at Chichén Itzá. This freestanding, humanoid sculpture served as a receptacle for* sacrificial items, perhaps human hearts.

have played different types of ball games with distinctive costumes, scoring rules, and court architecture. The Olmec apparently played a ball game at La Venta, but no formal court has been excavated such as those the Classic Maya used in their centers. The largest early Classic ball court, discovered at Kaminaljuyú, is one of more than 400 courts found in Maya country.

The action of Maya ball games would be in some ways familiar to modern spectators. In other ways, however, they would be completely mystifying. No written rules for playing the ancient game have survived, but European accounts from the 16th century provide some explanation. During the competition the ball bounced from player to player. Scoring occurred when it touched the opposing team's side of the floor or when it was driven through a ring high in the side of the court. The ball, made of solid rubber, probably weighed about eight pounds. The angle of the ring, the weight of the ball, and the rules for handling it made the game more difficult than many modern team sports. Players could not throw the ball by hand, but they struck it with their elbows, wrists, or hips.

A stone yoke, which Classic Maya ballplayers wore around their waist as protection. The average yoke measured 18 inches long and 12 inches wide.

Ballplayers wore leather or cotton pads to protect themselves against the bruising blows that the heavy ball might inflict. The players covered their knees and elbows with extra padding because these body parts received the greatest impact when players threw themselves onto the stone or plaster floor when striking a low ball. Classic Maya ballplayers also wore an elaborate yoke at the waist to protect the groin and chest. In contrast, Chichén Itzá ballplayers did not wear yokes. They did grasp a handstone—a flat, boxlike object—probably to protect their hands and to steady themselves when they kneeled to the floor. The Maya prized this equipment. It may have been passed down within families, as in the case of the equipment the Hero Twins received from their father.

The ritual sport tested the athletes' skills and entertained spectators, giving them a chance to gamble. (A Spanish observer reported that in Aztec games
continued on page 81

THE FIGURINES OF JAINA

Just off the west coast of the Yucatán Peninsula lies the small island of Jaina. In the Late Classic Period of Maya history (700–900), Jaina probably served as a cemetery for the elite of several mainland Maya centers. The massive tombs built throughout the island were filled with ornaments and other objects for use by the deceased in the afterlife.

Among the most beautiful burial offerings that have been excavated at Jaina are hundreds of clay figurines of about 5 to 10 inches in height. The best-crafted figures were molded by hand, but some were mass-produced by using molds. The figurines were then painted in brilliant blue, yellow, red, green, and white pigments. Many of the figures have whistles fitted in their back or head or are filled with pebbles so that they rattle when shaken.

Most of the Jaina figurines depict Maya nobles and rulers dressed in various costumes, such as those of warriors and ballplayers. But some of the figures represent people or deities seldom pictured in other Maya works. For example, several figurines of dwarfs, who served as entertainers for the royal court, and of the moon goddess have been found at Jaina burial sites. These subjects were probably considered more appropriate for these small sculptures than for carvings and murals in massive monuments.

The creators of the figures also had more freedom to depict realistic facial features and poses than did Maya artists who produced public works to glorify their kings. Possibly miniature portraits of actual people, the Jaina figurines are among the most expressive artworks of the ancient Maya.

A Jaina figurine of a dwarf dressed as a warrior. Strung through his earlobes are paper strips that were worn by participants in bloodletting rituals.

This figurine represents a captive of war. His contorted body and howls of pain are evidence that he has been tortured by his captors.

A warrior wearing a costume and helmet made of feathers. In some Maya paintings, warriors dressed like jaguars are shown defeating fighters in this type of clothing.

Like many other Jaina warrior figurines, this figure's face is marked with swirls that suggest elaborate face paint.

A seated noble wearing ball-playing regalia, including a jaguar-claw necklace and a protective garment made from a jaguar hide.

Dressed in a traditional huipil and elaborate jewelry, this regal woman weaving on a loom probably represents the moon goddess.

In this figurine, a moon goddess embraces an aging god. Sculptures such as this were probably buried in the tombs of elderly men.

Through this figure's highly expressive features and posture, its maker communicated the bewilderment of a drunk old man.

Wearing armor, this seated lord is dressed for war. The detachable headdress beside the figurine is constructed from an arc of feathers above a monstrous mask of an animal skull with a large gaping mouth.

Right: With the headdress hiding the lord's human face, he becomes a terrifying figure.

A ruler seated on an intricately carved throne covered by a jaguar pelt. He wears earflares, a wide collar, and a three-paneled cape.

The lid of the sarcophagus of Pacal, who ruled the city of Palenque between 615 and 683. The carving on the lid shows the moment of Pacal's death. From below, the Maw of the Underworld is rising up to engulf the ruler. Above Pacal is the World Tree at the center of the universe. The image, thus, depicts Pacal's descent from Earth to the Underworld.

A drawing based on a carving from Chichén Itzá that depicts the aftermath of a ball game. At the right is the body of a member of the losing team. At the left is a victor holding aloft the severed head of the loser. Snakes and a tree spring from the neck of the body, symbolizing the life-giving effects of blood sacrifice.

continued from page 72

the scoring team not only won the game but also the spectators' jewelry and clothing. When the ball was driven through the ring, fans fled to avoid paying tribute, with winners in close pursuit.) But carved scenes at the Chichén Itzá Ball Court and other sites suggest that the ancient game was actually a ritual battle for life and death. Maya artists sculpted 84 life-sized players on 6 stone panels of the court walls. Each panel pictures a human decapitation.

In the gruesome scenes, two opposing teams of seven members each face one another. On the left, a victorious player holds a knife in one hand and the head of his defeated foe in the other. Streams of blood transformed into serpents spurt from the victim's neck. The headless foe kneels to the right of a ball bearing a death skull. The ball symbolizes the slain player's head and indeed there are other scenes in which the head of a decapitated person was actually used in the game. Above the ball are plants, representing the fertility assured by the sacrifice. The Maya believed that nourishing the gods with the most precious things humans had to offer—heart and blood—insured fertility.

The ball game was certainly played with this objective in Classic times and even later. On one level, the game supported the daily cycles of death and rebirth of the sun and Venus; on another level, the seasonal cycles of re-

A sacrificial knife that was recovered from the Cenote of Sacrifice. To the Yucatec Maya, these objects were known as U kab ku, *meaning "hand of the god."*

generation of maize fertility; and on yet another level, the continuing cycles of dynasties and the kings themselves. A king did not offer his own life, but by selecting a high-ranking captive as the sacrificial victim, he perpetuated all levels of death and rebirth. In life and in the *Popol Vuh*, Maya ballplayers symbolized death and the subsequent transformation and rebirth.

Priests practiced a different kind of ritual offering at the Cenote of Sacrifice of Chichén Itzá. Northern Yucatán has few rivers or lakes, and during the dry season fresh water must be gained from wells or from the natural limestone holes, called cenotes, which dot the landscape. Maya therefore settled around these natural wells, and the people of Chichén Itzá used one cenote for their water source. The second and more dramatic well became the most sacred shrine of Yucatán. From a temple at the edge of this sacred cenote,

priests cast both persons and valuables into the water as an offering to the Rain Gods. Spanish chroniclers called it the Cenote of Sacrifice because of the human sacrifices conducted there.

Offerings also included huge quantities of jade, in most cases deliberately smashed, as well as copper bells, wooden spear-throwers, textiles, pottery, stones, bones, and shells. Many offerings were manufactured in other parts of Mesoamerica and carried to Chichén Itzá along commercial trade networks. From Panama and Costa Rica, the Maya acquired gold artifacts. From the Guatemalan highlands came jade and obsidian, and from Mexico came copper treasures. The priests also ceremonially burned copal incense and rubber. Both offerings, which came from tree saps, were shaped into balls and effigy forms, painted blue, and studded with jade and shells before being offered to the Rain Gods.

Describing these practices in the 16th century, Bishop Landa wrote: "Into this well they had had and then had, the custom of throwing men alive, as a sacrifice to the gods in times of drought, and they believed they did not die though they never saw them again. They also threw into it many other things, like precious stones and things that they prized."

Centuries later, Bishop Landa's words were verified. In 1904, amateur archaeologist Edward H. Thompson lowered a steel bucket into the greenish black waters of the cenote to discover if Landa was correct. On April 12, Thompson dredged up a wooden object that he described as being "beautifully carved into the figure of a personage richly dressed. The face is covered with a mask of beaten gold." Thus, Landa's description had been confirmed. The extraordinary items recovered by Thompson and subsequent divers and archaeologists document almost eight centuries of political, economic, and religious change in Maya civilization. Some carved jades dredged from the muddy bottom are of Classic workmanship. One jade bead, probably carved at Palenque, bears a Maya date equivalent to A.D. 690. Gold discs from the Toltec-Maya era depict Toltec and Maya confrontations. On one, two Toltec warriors attack a pair of fleeing Maya. The Toltec's glorification of military actions suggests that they consecrated the sacred cenote for their purposes.

Among the wooden objects taken from the cenote was the handle of a

A detail from the Dresden Codex *(a Maya book) that shows the planet Venus as a warrior (center). This Venus almanac scene prophesies drought, and Maya farmers must pray to Chacs, or Rain Gods, for their crops.*

sacrificial knife, carved with two inter-
twined serpents that are feathered
around the eye sockets. Thompson described the serpents' bodies as quetzal
green, with red eyes and white teeth.
The open jaws of one serpent hold a
chipped-flint blade. In the Yucatec
Maya language, such knives are called
U kab ku, hand or arm of the god.

Patrons of the holy well were the
Chacs, benevolent Rain Gods who re-
sided at the four corners of the world:
the Red Chac in the east; the White
Chac in the north; the Black Chac in the
west; and the Yellow Chac in the south.
For maize farmers, Chacs were primary
deities of life. The Dresden Codex pictures four Chacs prophesying good and
bad times.

Actually, Chacs represented a great
deal more than rain and good or bad
times. The Maya placed mask panels
with long curling noses on monumental
buildings as symbolic, repetitious, visual chants to the gods. Chacs joined
eagles, jaguars, and serpents as symbols of the religious and political system
in northern Yucatán.

Within this system, the glories of
Chichén Itzá and its Toltec-Maya rulers
vanished in chaos near the end of the
13th century. Tula also fell and the
shock waves were felt in far Yucatán—
similar to the effect on the Maya lowlands of the collapse of Teotihuacán
centuries earlier. The Yucatec Maya
may have eventually accepted the Tol-
tecs from Tula, but they despised the
Itza, calling them tricksters and ras-
cals, "foreigners . . . who speak our

language brokenly." After settling
Chichén Itzá, the Itza had founded
Mayapan in Katun 13 Ahau (A.D.
1263–83). When an Itza lineage named
Cocom seized power at Mayapan, this
center replaced Chichén Itzá as the Yucatán capital, about 1283.

A central character in this turning
point in Maya history was Hunac Ceel,
a Cocom noble who performed a dramatic and daring deed at the sacred
Cenote of Sacrifice. During ritual offerings, victims still alive at midday were
rescued in order to deliver the gods'
prophecy. Once when no survivor
brought the prophecy for rain or
drought, Hunac Ceel dived into the
well to get it himself.

An astute politician and wily adversary, Hunac Ceel ruled Mayapan and
allied with the ruler at Izabal. The Book
of Chumayal records that Chac Xib Chac,
ruler of Chichén Itzá, kidnapped the
bride of Izabal's ruler during the wedding festivities. Supported by Mexican
soldiers, Hunac Ceel led the war for revenge and sacked Chichén Itzá. Sculptures from the Temple of the Warriors
were deliberately thrown down and
treasures were looted. In Kutan 8 Ahau,
the Itza abandoned their city and traveled south to the deserted forests of the
Petén. There they made a new home at
Tayasal, an island in the lake that bears
their name—Petén Itzá. (Today, Tayasal is covered by Flores, chief city of
northern Guatemala.)

The Itza carefully planned Mayapan
to defend against military attack. A high
wall, with openings for access to the

city, protected it. They built no ball courts and only a few temples. A shoddy imitation of the Chichén Itzá Castillo pyramid, constructed with crudely cut stones, rises in the center of Mayapan. The descendants of Hunac Ceel ruled Mayapan and controlled Yucatán for nearly 250 years (approximately 1200–1450). Consolidating their empire, they made marriage alliances with ruling families of subordinate states and forced their chiefs to live at Mayapan. The Itza-centralized government administered a city of approximately 12,000 citizens. They lived on tribute goods from the vassals of the native princes whom the Cocoms held hostage in their capital.

Tulum, on the east coast of Yucatán, is one of the best-preserved remains of the Mayapan period. On a rocky cliff overlooking the sea, Tulum is defended from the land side by a stone wall; within the wall vessels could land on a small beach. The spectacular site is still a landmark to mariners.

During an ill-omened era, Katun 8 Ahau (1441–61), fate deserted the Itza. Revolt erupted at Mayapan led by the Mexican lineage Xiu who, like the Co-

A view of Tulum, a coastal landmark for navigators.

coms, claimed an ancestral seat at Tula. They slew the ruling Cocom and all his sons, except one away on a trading trip to Honduras. After this revolt, the Cocom empire dissolved into regional states with petty chiefs fighting for power.

Ironically, the last major event in Yucatán history before the Spanish conquest involved a pilgrimage to the Cenote of Sacrifice. To appease the gods who had afflicted his land with many calamities, Ah Dzun Xiu, ruler of Mani, began a sacred journey. He requested safe conduct from Nachi Cocom, ruler of Sotuta, through whose province the pilgrims had to pass. The Xiu ruler feared Nachi Cocom's wrath because Ah Dzun Xiu's great-grandfather had played a role in the slaying of Nachi Cocom's great-grandfather, final ruler of Mayapan.

Nachi Cocom promised them safe passage, all the while plotting revenge. When the pilgrims arrived, Nachi Cocom invited them to a royal banquet, at which the Cocoms killed all their guests. This massacre ignited old hatreds, which would prevent a united native stand against invading Spaniards. Exhausted by civil war, betrayed by some of their royal houses, and decimated by disease, the fragmented Maya fell prey to the better-armed Spaniards.

The Postclassic history of the southern highlands Maya parallels that of Yucatán. The Mexicanized Maya groups that culminated the fortunes of Yucatán also controlled the fate of the southern

A Guatemalan Maya man photographed in 1937, balancing his burden with a tumpline (strap) about his forehead. Before the Spanish brought horses and donkeys, the Maya carried loads in this way.

Maya. On the eve of the conquest, many independent nations existed, the Quiché and Cakchiquel being the greatest. They were probably descendants of the Putun Maya who had entered the highlands about 1200 and gradually forged a Toltec-type state. The *Popul Vuh* chronicles the Quiché's rise to glory. Claiming descent from Tula and Quetzalcoatl, the conquerors occupied mountainous strongholds as they conducted raids and eventually subjugated local people. In the 15th century, during the reign of Gucumatz (Feathered Serpent), the Quiché founded a new capital now known as Utatlán. The chronicles praised Gucumatz: "The nature of this king was truly marvelous, and all the other lords were filled with terror before him. And this was the beginning of the grandeur of the Quiché." Gucumatz's successor, Quicab, also extended the Quiché kingdom: "He made war on them and certainly conquered and destroyed the fields and towns of the people of Rabinal, the Cakchiquel. . . . One or two tribes did not bring tribute, and then he fell upon all the towns and they were forced to bring tribute." In about 1470 the Cakchiquel retaliated, and after establishing their capital Iximche, they began a new cycle of conquests of former Quiché areas. The *Annals of Cakchiquels* reports that people were slaughtered and their leaders captured and sacrificed. The aggressive Cakchiquel seem to have extended their conquests until the Spanish invaders arrested their power.

During the six centuries of the Postclassic era, all was not war and chaos. Trade brought steady wealth from the sea. One dependable trade item from Yucatán was salt, for one of the largest deposits in Mesoamerica lies along its northern coastline. Most of the salt consumed by the Maya, which was critical for their dietary, medicinal, and ritual purposes, came from these salt flats. For example, if Tikal had 45,000 citizens at its height in the Late Classical Period,

the minimal need for that community would have been 131 tons of salt per year. Since there are no salt sources anywhere near it, this salt had to be transported from distant regions. Most scholars agree that at the height of the Classic Period, around 800, the Maya lowlands had a population of at least 5 million whose minimal need was 40 tons of salt per day, or 14,600 tons per year.

Lucrative salt sources were a major objective of the Putun and clearly, the Itza's control of the salt beds and coastal trade networks provided the economic foundation for their political power. In their great seagoing canoes they skirted the low peninsular shoreline, carrying obsidian, copper, and fine textiles from the Gulf Coast to Yucatán. They·traded for salt and honey, then continued south to Honduras for stone metates and axes.

When the Spaniards arrived in the 16th century, they were impressed by the size and extent of the Yucatecan salt works. The earliest account comes from Bishop Landa in 1566: "There is a marsh in Yucatán worth recording, for it is more than seventy leagues long and is entirely salt. . . . This marsh is saline for God has made there the best salt which I have ever seen in my life." The Spanish conquerors took over these salt beds, which throughout history remained the largest salt-producing area in Mesoamerica. The Spaniards conquered the Maya city-states, but Maya culture and the count of katuns continued. ▲

A woodcut depicting Spanish conquistadores abusing their Indian bearers. The Spaniards had little respect for the economic and political accomplishments of the civilizations of native Mesoamerican peoples.

CONQUEST
AND
CONTINUITY

A Maya priest who added passages to one *Chilam Balam* history apparently predicted the disastrous appearance of foreigners before the event.

Eat, eat, thou hast bread;
Drink, drink, thou has water;
On that day, a blight is on the face of
  the earth.
On that day, a cloud rises,
On that day, a mountain rises,
On that day, a strong man seizes the
  land,
On that day, things fall to ruin,
On that day, the tender leaf is
  destroyed,
On that day, the dying eyes are
  closed,
On that day, three signs are on the
  tree,
On that day, three generations hang
  there,
On that day, the battle flag is raised,
And they are scattered afar in the
  forests.

The Maya actually met their first Europeans in 1502 when Christopher Columbus and his crew encountered a large Maya trading canoe near the coast of Honduras. Columbus's teenage son later reported that the ship was carved from one giant tree trunk. These Spaniards seized the canoe and rifled the cargo, which included copper axes; yellow stone hatchets; wooden war clubs studded with flints; pottery; and colorful garments of woven cloth. When cacao beans (money for the Maya) spilled on the floor, the Maya scrambled to save them "as if they were their eyes." Eventually, the Spaniards freed the canoe but detained its captain for a guide.

The invaders realized that this canoe belonged to a rich trading network. The wealthy merchant, his serfs, and the valuable cargo represented the type of sophisticated civilization that Columbus and other Europeans had been seeking. Maya reaction to this violent experience with the Spaniards is unknown, but surely the towering sails and arrogant aliens impressed them.

In the 16th century, soldier-chronicler Bernal Díaz del Castillo described two major goals of the invading Spaniards: "To bring light to those in darkness, and also to get rich." These goals guided the Spanish colonial system for the next three centuries as ruthless conquistadores and their descendants demanded land and labor, while priests forced Indians to embrace a new god.

The Yucatec prophet Chilam Balam had predicted the Spanish arrival long before it occurred: "The raised wooden standard shall come! Our lord comes, Itza! . . . Receive your guests, the bearded men . . . the bearers of the sign of God, lord!" But most Maya did not welcome the conquerors. Many Maya preserved their old ways; some remained independent; others fled. Rebellions were always crushed, and the Maya remained in bondage. The long, brutal conquest lasted almost 200 years before the last Maya stronghold disappeared.

The conquistadores' guns helped them to subdue the Indians, but perhaps the Spaniards' best weapons were the European diseases they transmitted to Mesoamericans. Having never been exposed to these illnesses, the Maya had developed no immunities to them. Exposed to these lethal viruses and germs, many Indians fell ill and died. The pestilence that may have been smallpox "rotted their bodies with a

Pedro de Alvarado, a lieutenant in Hernán Cortés's army, began his campaign to conquer the Maya on December 6, 1523. Alvarado's invasions of Indian villages were merciless. He burned villages and murdered the inhabitants throughout Guatemala.

great stench so that the limbs fell to pieces in four or five days." Epidemics often decimated armies and entire populations.

The Spaniards also shrewdly played Maya enemies against one another. On the eve of the conquest, the Guatemalan Maya were divided into warring groups, the Quiché and Cakchiquel being the most powerful. Having conquered the Aztecs in 1520, Hernán Cortés dispatched his lieutenant Pedro de Alvarado to conquer the Guatemalan

Maya late in 1523. The Indians called cruel, handsome Alvarado "Tonatiuh," the sun.

According to historian Bartolomé de Las Casas, Alvarado's Maya campaigns were ruthless: "He advanced killing, ravaging, burning, robbing and destroying all the country . . . under the pretext that the Indians should subject themselves to such inhuman, unjust, and cruel men, in the name of the unknown King of Spain, of whom they had never heard." Tecum, honored captain of the armies of the Quiché, fought Alvarado's forces in a battle that decided the fate of the Quiché Maya. A Quiché chronicle captures the battle's drama: ". . . the head of horse (Alvarado's) was taken off by Captain Tecum . . . Tecum was pierced . . . thus he went down that day before heaven. . . ." Tecum, the king's grandson, had dressed royally for battle. He wore three crowns fashioned from gold, silver, diamonds, and pearls, and appeared to be covered with green shimmering quetzal feathers. When Tecum fell, Alvarado and his soldiers gazed in awe upon their gallant enemy, and they named the site Quetzaltenango in memory of the quetzal feathers that adorned him and ". . . because a great captain died." The Quiché said the sun turned red and the water became a river of blood from the Quiché who died.

After the battle, the Quiché sued for peace and later invited Alvarado to Utatlán, their capital. The Indians plotted to torch the city once their enemies arrived, but Alvarado suspected a trap

A painting by modern-day artist Melvin E. Kester of a Maya nobleman holding a ceremonial bar.

and escaped Utatlán just in time. The Spaniards rallied and attacked the city. Then Alvarado ordered his men to burn the city because he considered it to be "a very strong and dangerous place." Alvarado also had some captured leaders burned alive.

When Utatlán fell on April 4, 1524, the Quiché suffered their final defeat. Alvarado baptized the surviving Maya princes and gave them Christian names. One was named Juan Rojas; for more than 450 years, each generation of his descendants has passed on this name to a newborn Quiché prince.

In contrast to the fighting Quiché, the Cakchiquel aided the Spaniards. However, the Cakchiquel soon became disillusioned with Spanish rule and rebelled against their former allies. According to a Cakchiquel account, Alvarado forced the chiefs to surrender their gold with the threat: "If you do not bring me the precious metal in all your town . . . I shall burn you alive and hang you." With the Cakchiquel defeat, the Indians lost their independence and suffered the yoke of economic exploitation by the foreigners. By 1527, the Spaniards had founded a new capital in the subdued highlands, and then turned their attention to the Maya in Yucatán.

The conquest of Yucatán took much longer than that of the southern Maya. After Columbus's encounter with the trading canoe, Spanish explorers had probed the coast of Yucatán from their base in Cuba. In 1517 an expedition led by Francisco Fernández de Córdoba,

discoverer of Yucatán, landed at Champotón. The Maya fought bravely even though the Spaniards must have been a strange and frightening sight with their horses, "thunder sticks," and fierce dogs. Nevertheless, the natives inflicted heavy losses on the better-armed Spaniards. Córdoba himself received 33 wounds and later died.

In 1519 another expedition commanded by Hernán Cortés landed at Cozumel. Accompanying Cortés were Bernal Díaz del Castillo, Francisco de Montejo, and Pedro de Alvarado, who played vital roles in the conquest. Cortés did not have permission from the Spanish crown to conquer and colonize Yucatán. In 1527, Montejo returned from Spain with a royal decree authorizing him to take possession of that land in the name of God and the king of Castile. Doing so proved to be a 20-year struggle led by Montejo, whose title was adelantado, and his son, Montejo the Younger.

The adelantado also landed at Cozumel Island, where the ruler Naum Pat offered friendship. Montejo then moved to the mainland. To quell mutiny among his troops, Montejo later set fire to his ships to prevent his soldiers from returning to Cuba or Spain. Then he set out with a small army of 125 soldiers to subjugate northeastern Yucatán villages. One Spanish witness described a vigorous Maya attack: "The Indians appeared with all the arms which they use in the wars: quivers of arrows, poles with their tips hardened by fire, lances with points of sharp

Indians attacking and killing the members of a Spanish landing party.

flints, two-handed swords of very strong woods inset with obsidian blades, whistles, and beating the shells of great turtles with deer horns." After more than 1,200 Maya were killed, the chiefs surrendered. Despite this victory, the adelantado ended his first attempt to conquer Yucatán in late 1528 when, after he failed to rendezvous with reinforcements, he returned in desperation to New Spain (Mexico).

The Spaniards' second invasion of Yucatán lasted from 1531 to 1535. Montejo sent his son to conquer the northern provinces. Montejo the Younger established the first *ciudad real* (royal city) at Chichén Itzá and then divided the nearby towns and villages among his soldiers, each Spaniard receiving the services of 2,000 or 3,000 Indians. Meanwhile, the adelantado had advanced inland to the Xiu province of Mani where the ruler, Tutul Xiu, welcomed him. Throughout the conquest, the Xiu supported the Spaniards.

Again Montejo's invasion of Yucatán collapsed when his disheartened soldiers deserted to join the conquerors of Peru who were gaining rich rewards. After fighting through northern Yucatán for seven years, the Spaniards had found only enough gold to fill a few helmets.

The weary, disillusioned adelantado entrusted the third attempt to conquer Yucatán to his son. In 1541, Montejo the Younger reached the ancient ruins of Tiho where he founded the city of Mérida. The ruler of Mani pledged his allegiance to the Spaniards. Since the fall

of Mayapan a century earlier, the Xiu province of Mani had been the most powerful political unit in northern Yucatán. When it submitted peacefully to the Spaniards, other western provinces followed suit. In contrast, Sotuta's ruler, Nachi Cocom, led an attack against Mérida, but he was defeated. Montejo the Younger then moved into the eastern part of the peninsula to subjugate Sotuta and the eastern provinces. Many Maya died in the bloody campaign. Savage war dogs tore defenseless natives to pieces. Some Indians died of starvation because they had no chance to plant their fields or replace the food that the Spaniards took from them.

One November night in 1546, the eastern Maya made their last united stand. The date was 5 Cimi 19 Xul in the Maya Calendar. (Cimi means death, and Xul means end; perhaps this date was chosen to symbolize the death of the Spaniards and the end of their Yucatecan rule.) The Maya crucified some Spaniards and killed others by slow torture. After defending their town fiercely, the Maya carried on guerrilla warfare from the bush. Some undoubtedly went to the distant and still free Petén Itzá. After four months of conflict, the Spaniards defeated the coalition of the eastern Maya chieftains and completed the conquest of Yucatán.

The Maya of the Yucatán peninsula held out longer against the Spaniards than any other group in Mesoamerica. Cortés conquered the Aztecs in only 2 years, but it took the Montejos 20 years

The Franciscan order's Church of St. Francis in Guadalajara, Mexico. The Spanish crown charged the Franciscans with the responsibility of converting the Indians to Christianity. By compelling the sons of nobles to learn Catholic tenets in monastic schools, the Franciscans trained native teachers who could be placed in local schools.

to conquer the Maya. Even in 1547, the Spanish victory was incomplete. The Maya who had fled south to Petén Itzá would not be brought under Spanish control for another 150 years.

The conquistadores had killed approximately 500,000 Maya, but natives still greatly outnumbered the Span-

iards. The invaders established control through their institutions of Crown and church. The Crown assigned Indians to Spanish overlords, called *encomenderos* in the *encomienda* system, which forced Indians to labor and to learn Christian doctrines, a system that disrupted Maya land use. Prior to conquest, families shared land and its products. For the Maya, handling their daily food was to hold the sacred in the palm of the hand. In contrast, the Spaniards saw the land's products as a means of making profits. Encomenderos exacted tribute from Maya laborers: woven cotton, salt, honey, and wax to export to New Spain.

Four Spanish towns dominated the peninsula: Campeche on the west coast, Valladolid to the east, Salamanca de Bacalar to the south, and Mérida, which became the seat of the royal government. Town officials collected taxes, supervised commerce, and enforced laws. By 1549, they administered some 178 Maya communities from Mérida and Campeche and controlled others from Valladolid and Bacalar.

Priests of the Order of St. Francis established church control, compelled Indians to accept baptism, and placed nobels' sons in monastery schools. Later, in village schools, these lads taught children and adults Christian doctrine and obedience to Spanish authority. In villages, Franciscans also supervised elections, administered funds, enforced regular church attendance, and charged the Indians for ritual services.

Friars further disrupted Indian lives by concentrating the scattered settlements into centralized locations that were more convenient for the clergy to visit. After ordering Indians out of their homes, friars burned their homes, fruit trees, and few possessions. Dazed and weeping Indians were herded off to new sites. Many died from hunger and exposure. This procedure created tensions between the priests and the encomenderos. Local encomenderos cursed the interfering friars who dared to move "their" Indians around the countryside without their permission. They also resented the friars' defense of the Indians against encomendero brutality. One cleric concluded, "It costs more to kill a cow or a horse in Yucatán than to kill an Indian."

In the midst of the conflict stood Diego de Landa, first *ministro provincial*

In 1562, Spanish official Diego de Landa led a three-month inquisition to punish Maya who were secretly practicing their native religion. The Spaniards' methods of torture included flogging their victims and burning them with melted wax.

of Yucatán. Landa boldly denounced the Spanish settlers' brutal treatment of the Indians. He also zealously vowed to eradicate Maya religion. When rumors spread that some Maya were secretly practicing ancient rituals (including two sacrifices at Chichén Itzá's Cenote of Sacrifice) and worshiping idols, Landa's friars tied the accused men's wrists together and hoisted them from the ground. Indians who refused to confess had great stones attached to their feet and were left to hang. Others were flogged and splashed with burning wax.

More than 4,500 Indians were tortured during the 3 months of Landa's inquisition, and 158 died. Landa defended his violence toward Indians on the grounds that such treatment was necessary to save their soul. Later, when Francisco de Toral, first bishop of Yucatán, investigated Landa's actions, the Indians denied their confessions. Accused of exceeding his authority, Landa was recalled to Spain to face the royal Council of the Indies in 1564. Years later, he was exonerated, and in 1572 Philip II appointed him second bishop of Yucatán to replace his old adversary Toral, who had died. Today, Landa remains controversial. Detractors denounce his actions, especially his burning of 27 sacred hieroglyphic books on July 12, 1562. Landa contended that "as they contained nothing in which there was not to be seen superstition and lies of the devil, we burned them all . . . which caused them great affliction." Defenders praise his *Relacion de*

las cosas de Yucatán, one of the most valuable sources on Maya culture and history.

By the time Landa died in 1579, a new Spanish-Maya society was emerging in which Maya lords became cultural middlemen. Before conquest, elite families provided leaders: The Xiu ruled in Mani, the Cocom in Sotuta, and so on. After conquest, native nobles governed rural Indians under orders of the Spaniards, who clustered in cities. Mérida remained the political, economic, and cultural capital of the Spanish province. Indians labored on the encomiendas and tended their milpas. They built massive Roman Catholic churches and gradually blended old gods with Christian saints. In eastern and southern regions where Spanish control was weakest, many Maya rejected Christianity and practiced their ancient religion under traditional leaders called H-men.

This cultural blending continued for the next two centuries. Gradually, numerically increasing ladinos (people of Spanish descent) and mestizos (people of mixed Spanish and Indian descent) replaced Maya officials. Mérida remained the center of the ladino world, and by the 1800s an increasing population placed new pressures on land and labor. Maya milpas and Spanish cattle had long coexisted. But as cotton, sugarcane, and then henequen (a plant whose fiber is used for making rope) became important commercial crops, Indian communities were squeezed by expanding plantations, called hacien-

Workers photographed in the late 1880s at a sugarcane mill in Cuautla, Mexico.

das. Whereas the conquistadores enslaved the Maya militarily, the hacienda owners enslaved them economically.

In 1821, Mexico won independence from Spain. Yucatán became part of the new nation, but the relationship was uneasy and painful. Yucatec leaders threatened several times to secede from the nation. (Guatemala and other provinces chose complete separation.) The Maya were declared free, but the debt peonage system continued. Plantation stores gave workers supplies on credit, but they never earned enough wages to repay.

Haciendas had their own chapels, patron saints, and fiestas for natives, and the landowners controlled food, justice, and services that Maya community leaders had formerly provided. Despite the Indians' fierce struggle

against Spanish encroachment, they lost control over land, community affairs, and daily life. No longer able to work their community milpas, the Maya also saw the end of their system of self-government.

In 1847 the Maya rebelled in the Caste War and almost destroyed the Hispanic society that had dominated Yucatán for three centuries. In conflicts between 1835 and 1847, Maya soldiers were drafted to fight in revolutionary armies. Indians were promised land and reduced taxes if they would serve in government forces, but the promises were forgotten. Outraged veterans rebelled, using their military experience and arms to attack Mexican forces. They also purchased munitions from British Honduras, and began fighting in eastern Yucatán where Mexican control was weakest. Hacienda Indians near Mérida did not rebel; some joined ladino forces. Wealthy, educated Indian leaders mobilized men and materials from local communities. Jacinto Pat, Cecilio Chi, Jose Maria Barrera, and others demanded that the government correct injustices by abolishing debt peonage and fees for sacraments, restoring peasant lands, and applying laws equally to all citizens.

Both sides committed bloody atrocities. After the Mexican military sacked General Chi's ranch, he slaughtered the ladino families in the village of Tepic.

In retaliation, soldiers torched Tepic, shot Indians, desecrated the church, and dropped stones in the village well. Unable to save their families, Maya survivors watched helplessly. News of the violence spread like wildfire; Mérida and other settlements became hysterical armed camps. As ladino fear mounted, peaceful Maya paid for the rebels' actions. Suspicious militiamen burned small settlements near cornfields and tortured innocent people.

In March 1848, General Chi attacked Valladolid, forcing the ladinos there to evacuate. Three months later, the

A late-19th-century photograph of a hacienda administrator (seated, left), his clerk, and Maya farm workers.

Indians occupied four-fifths of the peninsula. The opposition held only Mérida, Campeche, and a few urban settlements. When the Indians reached the outskirts of Mérida, victory seemed certain. Fearing the worst, Governor Barbachano prepared to abandon Mérida, and veterans organized to protect the 100,000 citizens whose lives depended on them. Then scouts discovered that the Maya army had disappeared. For unclear reasons, the rebels had halted outside the city. The arrival of the rainy season had signaled the time to plant corn, and religious duty and family responsibilities commanded the farmers. One soldier described the sowing crisis: "The time has come for us to make corn planting, for if we do not we shall have no Grace of God (corn) to fill the bellies of our children." Despite leaders' pleas, war-worn men walked past burnt-out towns, gutted sugarcane fields, and cattle ranches in order to return home to wives, children, and cornfields. Rebel command was weak because each man provided for himself and gave allegiance only to his *Batab*, who led a small force. Therefore, the Maya were not a completely unified force.

The tide turned as ladinos received artillery, food, and money from abroad. Yucatecan counterattacks swiftly drove the dissidents back to the east past Valladolid. Throughout 1849 Yucatecan forces inflicted sharp military jabs, and rebel morale plunged. Defeat brought conflict within Indian ranks. Rivals murdered Generals Chi and Pat. With

Maya farmers plant their cornfields, or milpas. *During the Caste War between rebel Maya and Mexican soldiers, corn-planting season signaled disaster for the Indians' cause as Maya farmers had to abandon the fighting in order to tend their fields.*

A late-19th-century photograph of henequen harvesting. Known as "green gold," this plant, which is used in rope making, was grown on huge haciendas.

a handsomely embroidered sash at his waist and his machete at his side, Chi was buried in his native Tepic.

Meanwhile the Yucatec yearned for peace; four years of war had claimed almost half their population. A reduced labor force had cut the corn supply. The army corps were underpaid and demoralized—sick, starving men tracking a sick, starving shadow enemy. But some 80,000 rebels, hardened by suffering, rejected surrender.

New leaders turned the movement into a religious crusade, centered on the cult of the Speaking Cross. In 1850, Jose Maria Barrera, who had served as a lieutenant under General Pat, established headquarters at a cenote known as

Chan Santa Cruz (Little Holy Cross) near the present town of Carrillo Puerto. Some said this sacred place harbored a miraculous wooden cross that could speak. The cross told rebels to fight without fear, for God would protect his Maya children from enemy bullets. When ladino soldiers confiscated the cross and killed the ventriloquist who seemed to speak for it, a new cross communicated in writing signed by Juan de la Cruz (John of the Cross). The cross communicated by letter with officials, including the governor of Yucatán. Sermons signed by Juan de la Cruz reveal that he was associated with Christ.

An 1851 account described a Yucatecan attack on Chan Santa Cruz in which 2,000 prisoners were taken and 2 crosses were confiscated: "From all parts of the interior families come to Chan Santa Cruz with the aim of adoring the crosses, burning candles and presenting them with money, maize, and other things." The rebels continued to believe that the crosses spoke in the name of God, assuring them triumph. The rebels became known as the Cruzob (blending *cruz*, Spanish for cross, with *ob*, the Maya plural suffix). Sometimes carrying the Speaking Cross into battle, the Cruzob raided the frontier and repelled Yucatecan drives against Chan Santa Cruz. Military service was cumpulsory and every man older than 16 bound himself in devotion to the cross. To guard the shrine, garrisons of

150 men rotated through the year. Thousands of Cruzob were killed by bullets, starvation, and cholera. Yet they survived against a better-armed enemy, establishing a small military-religious cult. The cult of miraculous crosses spread like holy fire. In 1866 followers were reported at Tulum and other villages.

After the major hostilities ended, weakened rebels were unable to launch an offensive that threatened Mexican control of the entire peninsula. During the period beginning in 1876, the modern industrial age reached Yucatán, ending forever the hope of regaining a Maya kingdom. This was the age of the worst exploitation of Maya labor. Sugarcane plantations, located primarily in the eastern part of the state, were de-

American anthropologist Alan Burns (center) and his wife with members of the Tuyul family. The Tuyuls are Maya who reside in Mérida, Yucatán.

stroyed during the Caste War, and many were never reestablished. On the other hand, henequen production recovered after 1848 in the Mérida area. The political stability of Porfirio Díaz's rule (1876–1911) ushered in Yucatán's era of "green gold," as henequen was called. Wealth from henequen production created an age of railroads, attracted foreign investments, and expanded exports. The invention of the McCormick reaper-binder revolutionized the grain industry in the United States, which then needed cheap twine to bind wheat sheaves. As henequen profits soared, Yucatán became the richest state in Mexico. Plantation owners built great palatial homes that lined the Paseo de Montejo in Mérida.

Bypassed by these economic changes, the Cruzob insurgents continued their resistance until 1899. Then Ignacio Bravo, a 70-year-old Mexican general, conquered them and silenced the Speaking Cross. The defeated Cruzob dragged their wounded and dead back into the bush. Cornered and desperate, but still dangerous, they prayed to God and their refugee cross. Refusing surrender, they hid in swamps and secret places.

The Caste War officially ended on May 4, 1901, when General Bravo occupied Chan Santa Cruz. Victory did not restore Yucatán's lost territory, however, for the Mexican government created the Federal Territory of Quintana Roo in the peninsula's eastern zone. The new governor of Quintana Roo established a truce with the Maya.

They kept to themselves, avoided their former shrine city, and did not submit to federal authority. In a surprising move in 1915, federal troops abandoned Chan Santa Cruz and returned it to the Indians. The separatist Maya created small village clusters, each with its own Speaking Cross.

The Speaking Cross inspired the most successful Indian rebellion ever to take place in North America. Today the tradition lives on in many small villages. In 1971, American anthropolgist Alan Burns visited the village of X-Cacal in the area of the last stronghold of the rebel Maya. One hundred and twenty years after the Speaking Cross first appeared, Burns found that the cross speaks as a representative of God through "counsels," reworked historical accounts mingled with prayer. Fighting has ceased, but the Maya preserve their tradition. According to Burns, "Ceremonies are performed to honor the Cross; guard duty is carried out around the sacred temples; and discussions about antagonism between Mexico and the Maya nation are heard." The villagers often asked Burns if the United States would provide money and ammunition to help them reclaim their territory from the Mexicans. In X-Cacal thousands of Maya attend yearly ceremonies to hear scribes read the *Chilam Balam* books as well as the sermon-speeches of Juan de la Cruz. The Speaking Cross cult has become part of the sacred tradition that links modern Maya to pre-Columbian Maya society. ▲

Maya Indians Rosinda (foreground) and Virginia Apen weaving traditional Maya cloth.

6

MODERN MAYA

Modern Maya living in Mexico, Guatemala, Honduras, and Belize have fared differently in the 20th century because of the various government policies in those countries. In 1910, Mexico convulsed in a bloody social revolution. Seven years later, victorious revolutionaries wrote a new constitution that altered the structure of Mexican society. Mexico's revolutionaries rejected historic Hispanic supremacy, so they changed governmental treatment of the Maya. Instead of sending armies to conquer rebels, revolutionaries sent schoolteachers to integrate the Maya into the nation by educating them. An intrepid schoolteacher established a school at X-Cacal, the village where Cruzob still mounted guard.

Thousands of Mexicans perished in the revolution, which Martin Luis Gutzman described as a "fiesta of bullets." Yet the upheaval of Yucatán was almost bloodless. After the war, this region became the testing ground for experi-

ments in political organization, labor, and education reform. By 1924, Governor Felipe Carrillo Puerto had established in all major pueblos at least one grant to a farming collective known as an *ejido*. These grants were part of the revolutionary government's plan for redistributing land ownership throughout Mexico. A typical Maya ejido consisted of a village of farmers and their lands. In 1937, Mexico's president Lázaro Cárdenas also showcased Yucatán as he presided over the greatest event of agrarian reform in Mexico's history. Within only 2 weeks, hundreds of haciendas were transformed into 272 ejidos.

By the early 1930s, henequen prices had plummeted on the world market, and foreign competition had severely reduced Yucatán's former monopoly. Yucatán fell from being Mexico's richest state to being one of its poorest. Today, the Maya must earn supplementary wages from jobs in Mérida and

A classroom in one of the many Indian schools created by the Mexican government in the 20th century. Government schools serve to integrate the Maya into mainstream Mexican society.

smaller centers. Like many other Mexicans, the people of Yucatán also suffer from overpopulation, underemployment, chronic political unrest, and violence. Yet, the revolution made significant changes. It ended debt peonage and developed workers' political awareness. It also created hundreds of new schools and dramatic improvements in health and sanitation. Yucatán now seeks ways to reduce dependence on a single export, to increase industrialization, and to promote tourism to the ruins that adorn the peninsula.

The Guatemalan Maya have not fared as well as their relatives in Mexico. Approximately one-half of Guatemala's population are Maya who live primarily in rural communities. Guatemala has not undergone a social revolution. Consequently its social structure is essentially the one established following Pedro de Alvarado's 16th-century conquest. Since 1524, Indians have gradually lost their land, then been forced to work it for pitiful wages—by Spanish landowners, Catholic clergy, coffee barons, and finally the modern

Guatemalan army. Today, ladinos control middle-altitude settlements in alluvial valleys, pushing Maya farmers up onto steep, less fertile mountain slopes.

Guatemalan history has been marked by continuous conflict for land. Only between 1945 and 1954 were democratic governments able to accomplish agricultural reforms. President Jacobo Arbenz Guzman's land redistribution plan provoked United States intervention to protect holdings of the American United Fruit Company (UFCO). As Guatemala's largest landowner, UFCO had enjoyed tax-exempt privileges on its banana monopoly and had held exclusive rights on railroad and telegraph systems. Appropriately, Guatemalans dubbed the American company "The Octopus." Arbenz offered to compensate UFCO for their unused land, but the company rejected his proposal and enlisted the aid of John F. Dulles, U.S. secretary of state, and his brother, CIA director Allen Dulles. The U.S. State Department conducted a propaganda campaign to convince the public that President Arbenz was a Soviet sympathizer. The CIA and the U.S. Marine Corps assisted Colonel Carlos Castillo Armas in toppling the Arbenz presidency in 1954. Instead of supporting laborers' rights and democratic land reforms, the United States supported unscrupulous dictators after Arbenz's fall. Under their military governments corruption increased: Ballot boxes were stuffed; trade union leaders, students, and politicians were assassinated; and thousands fled the country in fear. Guatemalans today reap the "harvest of violence" from the seeds sown by the 1954 coup. The indigenous peoples remain the poorest and most exploited sector of the population.

Between 1960 and 1974, the economy boomed as coffee, cotton, and sugar exports increased. The elite grew richer while peasant laborers grew poorer. Each year, more than 300,000 Indians migrated to work on coastal plantations, where they lived in subhuman conditions. Thousands were trapped in debt peonage. Cristina, an Indian woman from a village in the Department of El Quiché, describes the misery during this period:

> When I was three, I began going with my parents to the south coast plantations for the cotton and coffee harvests. The first child in my family to be killed, died there because of the poison sprayed on the coffee plants. After my brother died, my mother, who was packing coffee, kept him on her back the whole day. She waited until she had weighed the coffee before she put him down, and we buried him in a hole we dug behind the shelter where we slept with the rest of the workers from our village. None of them reported my brother's death, because the boss would have fired all of us on the next day.

As the crisis over land and labor deepened, Guatemalan governments increasingly repressed revolutionaries fighting for equal rights. In 1978, Kek-

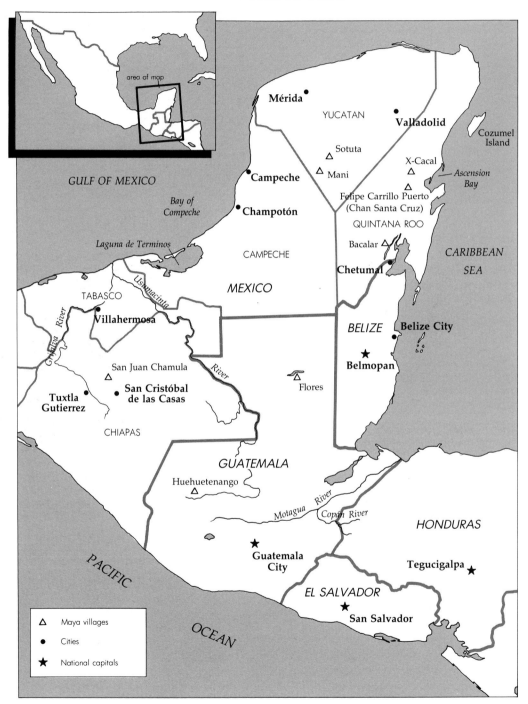

area of map

GULF OF MEXICO

Mérida •

YUCATAN

Valladolid •

Cozumel
Island

△ Sotuta

X-Cacal

△ Mani

△

Ascension
Bay

Campeche •

Bay of
Compeche

Champotón •

Felipe Carrillo Puerto
(Chan Santa Cruz)

△

QUINTANA ROO

Laguna de Terminos

CAMPECHE

Bacalar △

CARIBBEAN
SEA

Chetumal •

MEXICO

Usumacinta

TABASCO

Villahermosa •

BELIZE

Belize City •

Grijalva River

River

San Juan Chamula
△

△
Flores

Belmopan
★

**San Cristóbal
de las Casas** •

**Tuxtla
Gutierrez** •

CHIAPAS

GUATEMALA

Huehuetenango
△

HONDURAS

Motagua River

Copán River

★
**Guatemala
City**

Tegucigalpa ★

EL SALVADOR

★
San Salvador

PACIFIC

OCEAN

△	Maya villages
•	Cities
★	National capitals

chi Indians were promised titles to their lands, but when peasants marched to the town hall to secure titles, heavily armed soldiers opened fire, killing more than 100 Indians. Thousands of people left their native communities to seek refuge with guerrilla groups organized in response to murders committed by the army and death squads. One guerrilla leader had been in the mountains for seven years. Carrying a letter protected in wrinkled plastic, he explained:

> My wife was always afraid that they [the army] were going to kill me. . . . I haven't seen her in six years. . . . I think she fled somewhere with the children. I have her last letter to me. She sent it three years ago and I save it because it's the only letter I have from her. When I wish for another letter, I take this one out and read it again. It says, "I need you."

Many people have also suffered when family members suddenly and mysteriously "disappeared." Attorneys and judges, fearful of assassination, dare not pursue such cases. Lawyers must assume false names to identify burned and mutilated bodies. Remains of union leaders, priests, students, and other victims are discovered daily in ditches, hidden cemeteries, fields, and city dumps. More than 400 teachers have been killed. Many schools are destroyed or abandoned, and children miss their education. There is little prospect that conditions will improve because the military will not yield power. Nevertheless, some still nurture hope.

A young Guatemalan soldier, photographed in the church bell tower of Nebaj, Quiché, with a 50-caliber machine gun threatening the town plaza.

For example, Isabel de Castanon published an open letter to her husband:

> Keep going! Fight to survive in that secret corner, and we will continue fighting for your freedom, because they will never, ever be able to make honorable men vanish into thin air, as if they were nothing.

In this chaotic civil war, citizens were caught between two thorns—the guerrillas and the national army. As guerrilla activity increased in Indian homelands, the army accelerated conscription of Indian youth in a policy called "the grab." Without warning, soldiers filled villages, sealed off roads, and searched houses, seizing young men between 15 and 21 years old. Fear of "the grab" drove some youths to join guerrilla bands.

Another hated practice was the army's formation of civil guard units in highland Indian communities. Armed with only sticks and machetes, civil guardsmen between 13 and 70 years old were expected to prevent guerrillas toting guns from seizing supplies and damaging roads. Luis Garcia explained how guerrillas terrorized his village:

> Sometimes we had to give them food and sometimes a little money, though my father had almost none to give. They threatened to kill us if he did not. Someone told the army that my father was helping the guerrillas, and one night four soldiers came to our house. . . . They beat him and then shot him and cut off his head. . . . After that the guerrillas came back to our house again, and this time they pointed a gun at me and stuck a knife to my throat and said they would kill me if I didn't join them. . . . So I walked to Mexico. I was fifteen and afraid to go by myself, but I had to go.

Months later, Luis reached Indiantown, Florida, where he lives with his uncle and aunt who also fled Guatemala.

Luis Garcia is one of 150,000 refugees who escaped from Guatemala; another 250,000 displaced persons within the country urgently need food, medical assistance, and money. At the risk of losing their life, thousands resist leaving their homes. Robert Carmack, an American anthropologist, tells the story of one brave man from Santa Cruz del Quiché, the ancient capital of the Quiché kingdom. In 1978, the 30,000 Maya there gained hope with the election of the first Indian *alcalde* (mayor) in more than 200 years. He was Andrés Avelino Zapeta y Zapeta, a farmer and carpenter. Carmack described him:

> I found much in Zapeta to admire, and I loved him. . . . Zapeta was proud to be an Indian, and said so openly. Most Indians of Santa Cruz try to hide the fact, hoping thereby to avoid in some small way the scornful discrimination heaped on them by a ladino-dominated society. His love of church, family, Indian culture, work, and virtue seemed so out of place in the world in which Guatemala was now living.

In 1980, Avelino Zapeta was assassinated as he walked to his fields with his family to hoe his corn. Carmack continues, "I write at this moment because I want to capture the heartache and the outrage that I feel. . . . Something dies in us with the cruel death of someone as good as the alcalde. . . . Deep inside I knew that the alcalde had been innocent."

A drawing by a Maya child depicting a Guatemalan army helicopter firing on villagers as they pray outside a church. During the late 20th century, thousands of Guatemalans have fled their country in fear for their life.

Shedding innocent blood in a country where more than one-half of the population is Maya increasingly becomes Indian genocide. This holocaust liquidated entire villages. The most infamous example of genocide in one village appears in the testimony of Ricardo Falla, a priest and anthropologist. In Huehuetenango, 352 people were killed on July 17, 1982. The pattern was similar to other massacres:

> At about 1:00 P.M., the soldiers began to fire at the women inside the small church. The majority did not die there, but were . . . taken to their homes in groups, and killed, the majority apparently with machetes. . . . Then they returned to kill the children, whom they had left crying and screaming by themselves. . . . Then they continued with the men. They took them out, tied their hands, threw them on the ground, and shot them.

The soldiers piled the bodies in the church and burned them.

Fearing sudden attacks, entire villages disbanded into groups of refugees. One such group of 84 people reached a colony founded by Chamula Maya near Guatemala's border. Fortunately, the refugees were resourceful farmers who had cultivated fields on land that they had received through the Arbenz government's reform program before they were forced to flee. Recognizing the refugees' skill, their Chamula landlords hired them to work for wages. The community cares for its newest members and treats them as equals. Their children attend school, and they receive medical benefits. Less fortunate refugees have been exploited. After surviving in the jungles and mountains of the border region, others died from hunger and shock soon after their escape to Mexico. Still, resilient survivors vow to rebuild their shattered life and someday to return home.

Guatemalan refugees and Chiapas Maya share a common heritage. Approximately 1 million Maya live in the Mexican state of Chiapas. Each community expresses its own view of mythology and history. Neighboring communities may speak different Mayan languages and have distinct customs. Their religion integrates Catholic and ancient Maya beliefs. In this new vision, Jesus, Mary, and the saints from the Bible merge with the Sun God and Hero Twins from the *Popol Vuh*. Chiapas Maya also share a history of conflict. They have preserved Maya traditions through cycles of conquest.

San Juan Chamula, a Tzotzil-speaking Maya community in the central highlands, comprises the largest Chiapas Indian group. Approximately 100,000 Chamulas are scattered throughout the state in more than 100 hamlets. Like other Indians, they raise maize and work as day laborers. Most must work on lowland coffee plantations or in nearby San Cristóbal for several months each year for extra money.

Chamula history parallels other Maya history. Spaniards employed Aztec soldiers to march on the Chamula. Bernal Díaz records that 1,000 Chamula warriors, armed with obsidian-tipped lances, defended their citadel atop sheer cliffs. The warriors dropped rotten fish, pots of boiling oil, and rocks on the Spaniards. Nevertheless, the invaders' sword prevailed in 1524, and Díaz received all Chamula land and tribute for his military service. The Chamula survived intact the subsequent centuries of oppression.

Bishop Bartolomé de Las Casas arrived in San Cristóbal in 1545 with a decree from King Philip II placing Maya communities under the Dominican order. Land titles were stripped from conquistadores such as Díaz. Dominicans pledged to convert the Maya and to protect them from exploitation. Soon the cross prevailed as Dominicans exploited Indians for labor and fees. Yet the Maya remembered Christian teaching. They also remembered their ancient Sun and Moon deities. Thus, the Sun/Christ and Moon/Virgin Mary integration evolved from 16th-century Catholic missionization.

Mexico's independence from Spain did not improve Chamula life. Indians revolted in anger and frustration but were suppressed, like the Yucatec peoples. Lack of land continues to pressure the modern Chamula. They remain land-poor while ladinos control commerce, as they have since colonial times. Thousands of Chamulas have dispersed to colonies like the one the Guatemalan refugees founded. They live and work throughout Chiapas, but return to San Juan, hub of their spiritual and political world, to trade and celebrate. They hold festivals for saints and gods at the Ceremonial Center. The Chamula believe the center of the universe is within the San Juan church.

The Chamula map their universe with the earth between the sky and Underworld. Earth lords and demons inhabit caves that lace the earth. Earth lords, who send rain amid lightning and thunder, are associated with dampness and darkness. The dead dwell in the Underworld. The Sun/Christ and

A Maya festival at the town of San Juan Chamula, located in Chiapas, Mexico. The Chamula believe that the center of the universe is within this church.

Moon/Virgin Mary dwell in the sky. The Chamula have a special kinship with the sun, which plunges into the Underworld and rises each morning. Creator of the world, giver of life, and divider of day from night, the Sun is called "Our Father." He is the son of the Moon, "Our Mother." For the Chamula, as for their ancient forebears, the Sun created the world three times and destroyed it because humans behaved badly. The creator changed them into monkeys. His fourth creation is always in danger of destruction. The Maya must defend it, therefore, from bad people and evil demons. Ultimately, they must keep San Juan Chamula, the moral center, free from foreign intervention and corruption. Chamula allows no outsiders to spend the night in its boundaries without permission from municipal authorities. A priest, doctor, and schoolteacher, all ladinos, are permitted to live in Chamula if they observe restrictions. No Spanish-speaking Mexican may live permanently or hold property within Chamula except for the Mexican secretary, who directs the state and national governments. Violators face fines and imprisonment.

The Chamula perform sacred duties during many festivals each year. Dignitaries known as "cargo holders" sponsor the celebrations and tend images of Christ, the Virgin, and the saints. They incur heavy expenses but earn high esteem. ("Cargo" in Spanish can mean "responsibility.") Carnaval, which the Indians name the Festival of Games, is the greatest, most expensive

A Maya woman grinding corn with a mano *(handstone) and* metate *(grinding slab). Many ancient Maya traditions survive today.*

fiesta. From Carnaval, cargo holders, Christ's helpers, take their title, "Passion." Villagers say, "When the Passion walks, Christ walks; when the Passion dances, Christ dances."

Many sacred and secular themes are orchestrated into this great ritual drama celebrated during Crazy February. The term *Crazy February* refers to the carnaval season immediately preceding Lent in the Christian calendar. The festival also relates to the winter solstice in the ancient Maya solar calendar.

Diego de Landa described the New Year's ceremonies observed in 16th-century Yucatán during the 5 unlucky days at the end of each 365-day haab year. During these "Lost Days," evil spirits walk the earth and the world turns upside down.

Preparations begin weeks before the festival. Passions move to their temporary homes in the Ceremonial Center. Assistants gather firewood, sacrifice bulls for the banquets, and sweep the marketplace and churchyard. Flower gatherers adorn altars and shrines. An army of people cook corn gruel and prepare thousands of bean tamales and other festive foods.

Thousands attend the five-day celebration. Principal officials are the six Passions who impersonate the Sun/Christ, when they personify good. Each Passion, addressed as "Lord of Heaven," is "bearer" of Sun/Christ's burden on earth. God returns to earth through the Passions who give three banquets. Thus, God feeds his Chamula children, all of whom are welcome to feast.

Passions also personify evil. Soldier Passions represent centuries of invad-

Brightly attired Maya men carrying flags at the Festival of Games in San Juan Chamula.

ing armies. The Chamula integrate Christ's crucifixion with Cortés's conquest of Mexico, the Caste War, and the Mexican Revolution. Clearly, the last conflicts exploited the Chamula. War symbols appear: flags, drums, and fireworks. The Spanish Lady Passions (played by men) represent the conquerors' mistresses. Wearing a dirty white Mexican wedding dress, each flirts as the "Stinking Woman" who betrayed her people.

Passions have many assistants including Monkeys who symbolize evil monkeys who, with demons, killed the Sun/Christ. Monkeys wear a bizarre "soldier" uniform of red-and-black coats, short trousers, and monkey-fur headdresses, complete with a tail. Carrying whips, they guard ritual personnel and police the merrymakers. In addition to official Monkeys, hundreds of unofficial monkeys roam the plaza, jokingly threatening to seize people, wrap them in their tails, and carry them off into the forest.

Shortly after midnight, the first Lost Day begins with the Dance of the Warriors around the sacred kettledrums. Passions watch as hundreds of men are captured and "recruited" for their army. Dancing and ritual running continue for about 12 hours, culminating with a great feast of beef broth, chili, tortillas, corn gruel, sweet rolls, and coffee.

Excitement mounts on the second and third Lost Days as the Dance of the Warriors continues and Passions' servants busily prepare food. The fourth day begins after midnight with a spectacular torch and lamplight procession to Mount Calvary. This sacred place, located outside the community center, is the most important of many cross shrines the Passions visit. The procession carries Christian meaning, and also represents invaders' defeat of the Chamula. All must present tribute in order to be admitted to the mountaintop shrine. The Dance of the Warriors continues, and a great feast begins around noon. Meanwhile, Monkeys recruit two teams for a mock battle between Mexico and Guatemala. As trumpets sound, armies charge each other, throwing hard pellets of horse manure. Cheering, laughing observers know the fight represents a 19th-century boundary dispute. When the "manure war" ends, soldiers rush to the sacred spring to drink.

Monkeys also supervise the assistants' gathering of old roof thatch. Carrying it to the Ceremonial Center, they spread it to form the "Path of Gods." When ignited, it blazes as the path of the Sun/Christ across the sky. Key officials run back and forth three times over the flames and coals. Through this fire walk, all become part of the dramatic moment when the Sun/Christ ascended and vanquished evil forces.

Landa described a similar ritual that the Yucatán Maya performed during the Lost Days, more than 400 years previously. "Each took his bundle of rods, lit it, and . . . put fire to the firewood, which burned high. When only the coals were left, they smoothed and spread them out; then . . . some of them began to walk unshod and naked . . . across the hot coals. . . . "

After the San Juan purification ceremony, the market resumes and bulls are baited and chased in the plaza. On the Fifth Day, people rest before returning home. Passions pray, seeking forgiveness for failings during the festival. At noon, they give a final banquet. When the demons have been defeated, the religious officials have atoned for the peoples' sins, and the new year sun has been set in motion, San Juan Chamula is safe.

The Chamula invest great time, energy, and expense in the Festival of Games. They say, "If we don't do it and do it properly, we will die." In a sense they are saying that the Maya have survived by fusing native and newcomer cultures. The festival replays chapters of history with a Chamula accent. They are also saying that the Maya have endured change by preserving traditional beliefs and ceremonies.

The Chamula set themselves at the center of the universe by performing their rituals. Chiapas Maya women also symbolically place themselves at this center through weaving. They weave the sacred world and wear it on ceremonial huipiles. While attending a saint's statue, a woman wears a ceremonial huipil made in the same pattern as the saint's huipil.

Huipiles have been draped on statues in churches for centuries. Weavers study these elegant models to learn traditional designs. Saints may also inspire

A detail of a woven Maya blouse, or huipil. *The pattern at the top indicates the path of the sun, the one below it indicates that the wearer has held a religious office, and the pattern at the bottom—a "toad's back"—is the weaver's signature.*

designs in women's dreams. A huipil well dreamed is truly beautiful. Women also create special huipiles for weddings, burials, and official events. These rectangular blouses bear elaborate geometric designs that represent cosmological elements including the sun, moon, and stars.

Weaving is a kind of language. Each community's distinctive style of dress identifies its members. Women arrange traditional designs according to per-

Two Maya women model huipiles. The Maya read the cultural codes woven into such blouses.

sonal taste and skill. The modern Maya read these cultural codes, just as the ancient Maya read the symbols on Lady Xoc's huipiles on the Yaxchilan Classic Period stela. Women have woven these designs for more than a thousand years, and they keep tradition alive by reworking ancient patterns, slightly varying form, size, and color combinations.

Line by line, sacred symbols are woven into Maya cloth. The weaver maps the movement of the sun (personified as Jesus Christ) through the heavens. To set the sun in motion, she repeats rows of diamonds. Curls on each side of the inner diamond represent wings, called butterfly. This is the symbol for the day sun. Diamond-shaped designs representing the universe have been sacred images since the Classic Maya Period. Lady Xoc wore this same motif in A.D. 709 during her bloodletting ritual.

A huipil encloses a woman in a sacred space. When a Maya woman puts on her huipil, she emerges through the neck opening symbolically in the center of a world woven from dreams and myths. As altars and crosses are ritually adorned with fresh flowers, the neck of the huipil is decorated with woven and embroidered flowers.

In addition to creating special huipiles, women also weave textiles for their families and for sale. They weave striped and plain white cloth for shawls, men's shirts, and children's clothes. A generation ago, all clothing worn by the highland Maya was hand-spun and handwoven, but today most men buy collared shirts to wear under their woven tunics. Women may purchase cloth for huipiles and embroider bright designs on them. Designs and fabrics may gradually change, but weavers continue to use the backstrap loom that has been functional for more than 2,000 years. This portable, easily stored loom allows them to use a wide range of techniques to produce many kinds of textiles.

Today, Maya women weave textile designs that have lasted more than 1,200 years. Even in Chiapas refugee camps, women continue weaving. In order to help support their families, they sell textiles. One woman explained, "Even though our designs are not the same, the act of weaving represents something important. It shows people on the outside that we want to live, we don't want to die. I don't want to stop participating in my culture."

In Maya culture, old patterns persist alongside new ones. Rural men make milpa and women weave, cook, and tend children. They pay homage to maize and pray for rain. Urban Maya in Mérida, Guatemala City, and Mexico City run computers, sewing machines, and other technological equipment. The Maya take from the modern world what they find useful. Even milpa makers listen to transistor radios, and traditional priests record age-old ceremonies on cassette tapes. As the Maya move into the 21st century, the outward symbols may change, but the inner spirit remains Maya. ▲

BIBLIOGRAPHY

Carmack, Robert M., ed. *Harvest of Violence: The Maya Indians and the Guatemalan Crisis.* Norman: University of Oklahoma Press, 1988.

Clendinnen, Inga. *Ambivalent Conquests: Maya and Spaniards in Yucatán, 1517–1570.* Cambridge, England: Cambridge University Press, 1987.

Coe, Michael D. *The Maya.* 4th ed., rev. New York: Thames and Hudson, 1987.

Meyer, Carolyn, and Charles Gallenkamp. *The Mystery of the Ancient Maya.* New York: Atheneum, 1985.

Morley, Sylvanus G., and George W. Brainerd. *The Ancient Maya.* 4th ed., rev. by Robert J. Sharer. Stanford, CA: Stanford University Press, 1983.

Recinos, Adrian, Delia Goetz, and Sylvanus G. Morley, trans. *Popul Vuh: The Sacred Book of the Ancient Quiché Maya.* Norman: University of Oklahoma Press, 1950.

Reed, Nelson. *The Caste War of Yucatán.* Stanford: Stanford University Press, 1964.

Robertson, Merle Green. *The Sculpture of Palenque.* 3 vols. Princeton: Princeton University Press, 1983–86.

Schele, Linda, and Mary Ellen Miller. *The Blood of Kings: Dynasty and Ritual in Maya Art.* Fort Worth, TX: Kimball Art Museum, 1986.

Stuart, George E., and Gene S. Stuart. *The Mysterious Maya.* Washington, DC: National Geographic Society, 1983.

Thompson, J. Eric S. *Maya History and Religion.* Norman: University of Oklahoma Press, 1970.

THE MAYA AT A GLANCE

CULTURE AREA   *Mesoamerica*

GEOGRAPHY   *Mexico, Guatemala, Honduras, Belize, and El Salvador*

LINGUISTIC FAMILY   *Mayan*

CURRENT POPULATION   *Approximately 5 million*

FIRST CONTACT   *Christopher Columbus, Italian, 1502*

GLOSSARY

archaeology The scientific study of the past life and culture of peoples, conducted by excavating cities and relics.

Carnaval The season or festival of merrymaking and revelry before Lent, observed especially in Roman Catholic societies.

cenote A deep natural well in limestone that holds groundwater; from the Maya word *tzonot*.

chacmool The statue of a reclining deity with flexed knees and hands holding a receptacle.

city-state A political unit in which an urban center controls the population in a rural, food-producing territory.

codex An ancient Native American manuscript, written in *hieroglyphic* symbols on prepared animal skins or tree bark and bound in panels.

cosmology The worldview of a specific people encompassing the relationship between humans, supernatural beings, and the natural world.

Cruzob The Maya term for believers in the Speaking Cross cult.

debt peonage A system whereby persons are compelled to perform labor for their creditors because of unpaid debts.

divination The act of foreseeing or foretelling future events or discovering hidden knowledge or the cause of illness.

dynasty A succession of rulers who belong to the same family.

ejidos Mexico's rural collective landholding units, created as an agricultural reform after the Mexican revolution.

encomienda A Spanish colonial institution that granted Spanish overlords (*encomenderos*) the privilege of collecting tribute and requiring labor from Indians. Encomenderos were responsible for converting their Indian laborers to Christianity.

genocide Deliberate, systematic extermination of a human population.

hacienda A large unit of land owned by a family wielding tremendous social, economic, and political power. Many Maya workers were exploited by hacienda owners.

hieroglyph (glyph) A written symbol representing an idea, object, syllable, or sound.

ladino A person of Spanish descent who follows Hispanic cultural practices.

lintel A horizontal piece of timber or stone over a door, window, or other opening that carries the weight of the wall above the opening.

mestizo A person of mixed Indian and Spanish ancestry who follows Hispanic cultural practices.

milpa A maize field.

obsidian A hard volcanic glass ranging in color from reddish brown to black. Obsidian can be easily worked to create razor-sharp edges on weapons and tools.

Olmec A Gulf of Mexico coastal lowland people whose civilization began before 1000 B.C. and who were the apparent inventors of Mesoamerican writing.

pectoral An ornament or breastplate worn on the chest.

Popul Vuh A manuscript that records the sacred and secular history of the Quiché Maya.

quetzal A crested bird of Central America with brilliant plumage, greenish upperparts and throat, and crimson underparts. The long, streaming tail feathers of the male may be more than two feet in length.

Quetzalcoatl A creator god, also known as the feathered serpent and the morning star.

Speaking Cross cult A religious movement that originated in Yucatán in the mid-19th century and centered around the belief that a sacred cross could speak and communicate sacred messages.

theocratic chiefdom A political organization ruled by a priest-king who interprets and represents divine will.

Toltec People from Tula in the Valley of Mexico.

Xibalba The underworld in Maya cosmology.

INDEX

PICTURE CREDITS

LAWANA HOOPER TROUT is professor of English at the University of Central Oklahoma. She received her B.A. from the University of Oklahoma, her M.A. from the University of Tulsa, and her Ph.D. in English from Northwestern University. In 1964, she was named National Teacher of the Year. Dr. Trout has edited 10 books, including 2 literature series for high school students that have been adopted as texts by many state school systems. She has also compiled the anthologies *Myth; Folklore;* and *Tales, Talk, and Tomfoolery* and written several articles. Dr. Trout has conducted workshops and institutes for secondary school and university teachers in the United States, Mexico, Canada, Europe, and England. From 1975 to 1990, she directed summer institutes in American Indian history for secondary school instructors and Indian reservation college teachers at the D'Arcy NcNickle Center for the History of the American Indian at the Newberry Library in Chicago, Illinois. She is a member of the National Humanities Faculty of Humanities, Arts and Sciences.

FRANK W. PORTER III, general editor of INDIANS OF NORTH AMERICA, is director of the Chelsea House Foundation for American Indian Studies. He holds a B.A., M.A., and Ph.D. from the University of Maryland. He has done extensive research concerning the Indians of Maryland and Delaware and is the author of numerous articles on their history, archaeology, geography, and ethnography. He was formerly director of the Maryland Commission on Indian Affairs and American Indian Research and Resource Institute, Gettysburg, Pennsylvania, and he has received grants from the Delaware Humanities Forum, the Maryland Committee for the Humanities, the Ford Foundation, and the National Endowment for the Humanities, among others. Dr. Porter is the author of *The Bureau of Indian Affairs* in the Chelsea House KNOW YOUR GOVERNMENT series.